ISLE OF WIG
RAILWAYS

The Cheapest way to see the Island.

A 7-day "All-Island" Season

Covers the 32 Isle of Wight Stations
(See Map, page 366).

Price, **11/-** 1st Class; **8/-** 3rd Class.
(Children under 14 half-price.)

TRAVEL WHERE YOU LIKE—
WHEN YOU LIKE—
AS OFTEN AS YOU LIKE.

These Tickets are issued from April 1st to October 31st, and are obtainable on demand, any day, at any S.R. Isle of Wight Station.

NOTE:—7-Day Season Tickets as above, and including Southern Railway Steamboats between Ryde, Southsea Pier Heads (Clarence & South Parade) and Portsmouth, 19/- 1st Class: 15/9 3rd Class rail and 1st Class boat.

Extract from 'Holiday Hints for 1938'. *Courtesy of Derek Priddle*

Southern Railway Season Ticket. *IWSR Museum Archives*

ISLE OF WIGHT RAILWAYS

A 'then and now' pictorial survey

Colin A. Pomeroy

Foreword by the late Sir Peter Allen
Former President of The Transport Trust

Past & Present Publishing Ltd

Also by Colin Pomeroy and available from Past & Present Publishing Ltd

The Bermuda Railway. Gone - But Not Forgotten (1993; ISBN 0 9521298 0 9)
Military Dorset Today (1995; ISBN 1 85794 077 6)

The 'then' station layout plans are from the collection of the
Signalling Record Society, whose help is gratefully acknowledged

First published in hardback as *Isle of Wight Railways, a 'then and now' pictorial survey*
by Silver Link Publishing Ltd in July 1991
Paperback edition first published in June 1993
New revised edition with colour published October 1996

British Library Cataloguing in Publication Data

A catalogue record for this book is available from the British Library

ISBN 1 85895 123 2

Past & Present Publishing Ltd
Unit 5
Home Farm Close
Church Street
Wadenhoe
Peterborough PE8 5TE
Tel (01832) 720440
Fax (01832) 720531
e-mail: pete@slinkp-p.demon.co.uk

Printed and bound in Great Britain

Contents

Foreword
to the first edition

by the late Sir Peter Allen,
Former President of the Transport Trust
and former Chairman of ICI plc

My first introduction to the railways in the Isle of Wight was in 1915 when I was 10 years old, and an interest was born which I have retained ever since. From those pre-Grouping days, I saw the system grow to its zenith before the Second World War and for the all too brief revival immediately afterwards. Then followed a steady

A lifetime of interest in Isle of Wight Railways lies ahead of young Peter Allen as, at the age of 10 in 1915, he stands proudly beside the FYNR's 0-6-0 Manning Wardle 'Q' Class locomotive 'FYN1' at Freshwater station.

decline, with the progressive closure of lines until all that remained was the Ryde Pierhead to Shanklin section. In true Island tradition, this rump of the formerly extensive system was modernised using second-hand cast-offs from the mainland, but at least a railway remained! Then, in 1971, the Wight Locomotive Society established a permanent headquarters at Havenstreet — an organisation with which I am pleased to be associated — and since then there has been a slow but progressive improvement in both the nationalised and the preserved lines, which will culminate this year in a physical link between the two with a joint station at Smallbrook Junction.

In spite of the closures, the first of which occured almost 39 years ago, many traces of the old lines remain and Colin Pomeroy has done an excellent job in methodically matching old photographs with the locations as they are today. It continues to surprise me that previously unpublished photographs of years gone by are still being found; thus this volume not only matches the scenes of past years with those of today, but also presents the reader with a selection of new pictures.

There have been many books devoted to the Island's railways and I am proud to have written what was probably the first of them; none, however, have sought to show the system in the manner now presented. I sincerely hope that this book will not only provide a link with the past but also provide an impetus to ensure that what remains, both operational and historical, will be enjoyed by future generations.

British Rail
Standard Class Pass
Holder MR COLIN POMEROY
between ISLAND LINE - ALL STATIONS

Expiring 2 1 MAR 1996
Unless previously recalled

No. DD 018770

ISLAND LINE
Authorising Office
and Location
RYDE ESPLANADE

Introduction
and acknowledgements

In bringing together this collection of photographs, I have attempted to capture the unique atmosphere of the 'Garden Island' and its once extensive railway system, both as it was and, as far as is possible, as it remains today.

It is now 25 years since steam last hauled a passenger or goods train on the Island — with the obvious exception of those running at the excellent Isle of Wight Steam Railway Centre at Havenstreet — and the passage of time, especially in the larger towns, is rapidly removing many of the buildings and artefacts that would otherwise be capable of linking together the railway system of the period 1862-1966 with the present.

I hope that this book will encourage those who are too young to remember much of the Island's old railway system to seek out these numerous links with history before it is too late and, equally, I hope that the book will bring back fond memories for those who were lucky enough to participate in the steam age and who, perhaps, stop and wonder what the Island still possesses of its railway heritage. Please remember, however, when seeking out today's relics of the railway era, that much of the closed elements of the system lie on private land and that permission should be sought before attempting to gain access thereto.

In taking the 'now' photographs, I have made every attempt to capture the same background scenery, from the same camera position as the photographers of old. However, readers will appreciate that some minor differences are inevitable and for these I offer my apologies. Hopefully, any such differences will not detract from the overall enjoyment of the book!

I would particularly like to record my thanks to Roger Silsbury for making available to me the Isle of Wight Steam Railway's photographic collection, for proof reading my original draft and for making so many helpful suggestions.

Additionally, I would like to place on record, in alphabetical order, my sincere thanks to those who have given me so much cheerful help and friendly advice in the bringing together of this book: Chris Ashworth, Tony Bennett, Andrew Britton, Tim Cooper, Nicholas Dicks, Terry Hastings, Isle of Wight County Council

Records Office, Isle of Wight County Libraries at Newport and Cowes, Paul and Jenny Schmid, Adrian Searle, Tony Sedgwick, the Signalling Record Society, Don Vincent, Rosie Westlake, John Winkles, BR Manager Isle of Wight, Ron Wyatt, and many members of British Rail's Network SouthEast 'Island Line'. I would also like to thank those not mentioned above, but credited in the text, who so kindly allowed me to use their photographs. I must also express my thanks to those who live along the abandoned lines today, and who have been so kind in allowing me access to their private property. Without their co-operation the writing of this book would have been impossible.

Finally, I must thank 'Binks', my wife, whose patience and understanding have made my task that much easier than it might have been.

Introduction to the 1993 edition
Since the taking of the majority of the photographs in 1990 and 1991, things have moved on apace on the Isle of Wight. Amongst the more prominent changes, the IWSR has achieved its ambition of running through to Smallbrook Junction, the Cowes Station site redevelopment has all but been completed, and Newport Tunnel has been altered to accommodate the new Ryde slip road off the Newport bypass. With minor amendments to the earlier text, the book has been updated to reflect these changes. Currently the future of the main line on the Island is being carefully considered - with the possibility of it being one of the first to be privatised. Could we once again see steam trains running to Ryde Pierhead - and even through a re-opened Ventnor Tunnel?

Introduction to the 1996 edition
Nearly five years have passed by since the 25th anniversary of the ending of steam-hauled operations by BR on the Island and the first edition of this book. The former London Underground trains still make their daily journeys between Ryde Pierhead and Shanklin, whilst the IWSR continues to impress all who visit it at its Havenstreet headquarters. Since the second edition of the book, the joint station at Smallbrook Junction has opened, and serves the trains of both operators, the IWSR halt at Ashey has re-opened, and the former Cowes Station site has continued to see major development; very little else has altered in railway terms. This, however, is about to change as the Island Line prepares for privatisation - with the pre-qualification document being issued by the Office of Passenger Rail Franchising on 26 April 1996 and the target date for the completion of the process being in October. Unlike mainland privatised rail companies, the Isle of Wight operator will control both trains and infrastructure (track, stations, etc).

The sight of trains running once more through Ventnor Tunnel is still very much a possibility, with the Ventnor Railway Association producing an impressive case for re-instatement of the line from Shanklin to Ventnor - following the former BR trackbed, but with a cut-and-cover tunnel at Wroxall to overcome the only major blockage of the old route.

With the addition of a selection of 'past and present' colour photographs, and some further updating of the text, the book now commemorates the 30th anniversary of the ending of 'main-line' steam operations on the Isle of Wight, whilst looking forward to the exciting railway future on the Garden Isle.

A brief history of the Isle of Wight railway system

Many books have already traced the history of the Island's railways in great detail and, in what is essentially a collection of photographs, I will not attempt to repeat that task yet again within these pages; however, a few brief details are necessary to set the scene.

The 4½-mile line of the Cowes & Newport Railway, from Newport to the town and port of Cowes, was the initial stretch of line to be opened, the first trains running along the attractive west bank of the River Medina in 1862. Two years later, the Isle of Wight Railway's line from Ryde to Shanklin saw its first services, being extended to the holiday resort of Ventnor by 1866. By 1875 the Island's three major towns of Ryde, Newport and Cowes were linked together by the Cowes & Newport and the Ryde & Newport Railways; by the end of the 19th century, all the lines had been completed: to Bembridge (the Brading Harbour Railway), Newport to Freshwater (the Freshwater, Yarmouth & Newport Railway), between Newport and Sandown (the Isle of Wight [Newport Junction] Railway), and to Ventnor West (the Newport, Godshill & St Lawrence Railway). This was the extent of the system when Grouping took the Island's railways into the Southern Railway in 1923, and remained essentially so when post-war Nationalisation followed 25 years later.

With the wonderful benefit of hindsight, it now appears that much of the railway expansion on the Island was carried out with the heart — in the form of steam mania — rather than the balance sheet as the main *raison d'être*. Certainly, in the days prior to Grouping, the lines struggled to make financial ends meet; however, after 1923 the services did improve and some of the problems associated with rural localities, increasing competition from road transport and indifferent locomotives and poor rolling-stock, were lessened.

One major problem throughout the history of the system was the one which is equally prevalent today in the commuter belts of Network SouthEast, when busy weekday rush hours contrast with the slack periods of weekends and off-peak travel — unequal utilisation rates for the rolling-stock. In the Isle of Wight's case, though, the problem was one of accommodating the surges of thousands of holidaymakers in the summer months — especially at weekends — and of having idle assets

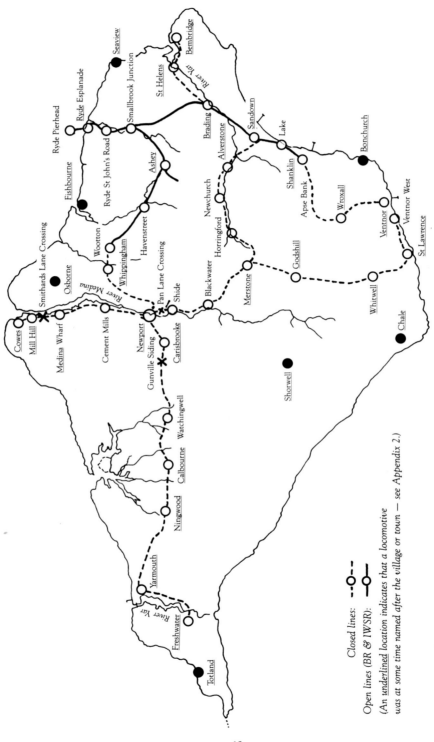

The Isle of Wight railway system

Closed lines:
Open lines (BR & IWSR):
(An underlined location indicates that a locomotive
was at some time named after the village or town — see Appendix 2.)

Résumé of opening and closure dates

Route	Approximate mileage	First service	Last service
Cowes to Newport	4½	16 June 1862	21 February 1966 (Pass)
			16 May 1966 (Freight)†
Ryde St John's Road to Shanklin	7¼	23 August 1864	Still in operation
Shanklin to Ventnor	4	10 September 1866	18 April 1966 (Pass)
			16 May 1966 (Freight)
Sandown to Shide	8½	1 February 1875	6 February 1956
Shide to Newport (Pan Lane)	1½	6 October 1875	6 February 1956
Smallbrook Junction to Newport	10	20 December 1875	21 February 1966 (Pass)**
			16 May 1966 (Freight)**†
Pan Lane to Newport	less than ¼	1 June 1879	6 February 1956
Ryde St John's Road to Ryde Esplanade	¾	5 April 1880	Still in operation
Ryde Esplanade to Ryde Pierhead	½	12 July 1880	Still in operation
Brading to Bembridge	2¾	27 May 1882	21 September 1953
Freshwater to Newport	11¾	10 September 1888 (Freight)	
		20 July 1889 (Pass)	21 September 1953
St Lawrence to Merstone	5½	20 July 1897	13 September 1952
Ventnor West to St Lawrence	1¼	1 June 1900	13 September 1952

Notes

Pass = Passenger service.

**Except the section Havenstreet to Wootton and to Smallbrook Junction, via Ashey — reopened in stages from 1971 by the Isle of Wight Steam Railway.

†Engineers' trains continued to work the section from Medina Wharf to Smallbrook Junction, mainly on electrification work, until 1967.

throughout the winter. If too much stock was held on the Island, a poor financial return was forthcoming away from the holiday peaks; if too little stock was available, maximum income could not be generated when the passengers wished to use the system. It was an insoluble problem, exacerbated by the Island's isolation and the inability to transfer equipment to and from the mainland without recourse to complex shipping operations.

The 1950s closures of the line to Ventnor West, the Bembridge branch, the line to Freshwater, the Newport to Sandown line and Whippingham station on economic grounds (and of Wootton station due to geological problems), all pre-dated the infamous cuts of Dr Beeching in 1966, when the Cowes to Newport and Ryde line and the line from Shanklin, beneath St Boniface Down, to Ventnor lost their services. The dubious economic arguments advanced in support of the closures, certainly of the Shanklin to Ventnor section of the system and, probably, of the Ryde to Cowes line as well, leave many Islanders and other railway enthusiasts totally unconvinced of their merit.

As the photographs that follow show, today's reminders of the Island's railway past are many, varied and wide-ranging. The original stations on the Ryde Pierhead to Shanklin line and the Isle of Wight Steam Railway's station at Havenstreet are the most obvious examples of the rich railway heritage of the Isle of Wight; at other locations, indications of former railway use vary from the virtual inability to spot even a gentle reminder of the past - as is the case at Carisbrooke - to perfectly preserved station buildings, with associated steam age archaeology, such as at St Helens and Watchingwell.

Of course, it has not only been the swingeing axe of the Beeching era which has transformed the trackside scenery. In many places, social changes have altered the backdrop to the passing of the trains beyond recognition, with new road layouts, extensive house and light industry building schemes, the closure of quarries and the demolition of time-expired factory sites and hotels all contributing to the changes that are apparent today. Nature, too, has played its part - where the track has been lifted, new growth has occurred, the passage of time eliminating all signs of the passage of trains! The severe storms of October 1987 and January 1990 also left their mark, as did the outbreak of Dutch Elm Disease in the 1970s, and in many places fine specimen trees which have watched over the island's railway system since its inception have fallen and been turned into logs. It is all these changes, combined with the changes in the railway itself, which make a comparison between the railway system 'then' and 'now' so fascinating.

Today, ex-LRT electric trains maintain BR's services between Ryde Pierhead and Shanklin, a distance of merely 8¼ miles, compared with the 55½ miles serving the Island in its heyday. However, even on this truncated stretch of the railway, changes still occur, and as recently as 1987 a new halt was opened at Lake, to serve the residential area between Sandown and Shanklin. I wonder what comparisons will still be meaningful in another 25, 30 or even 50 years time? I leave you to ponder and to draw your own conclusions, as we begin our tour of the Island at Ryde Pierhead.

Part 1

Ryde to Ventnor, and the Bembridge branch

Ryde Pierhead

Opened: 12 July 1880 **OS Map Reference: SZ 594936**

An information-packed view, taken from the old Ballroom on a summer's day during the inter-war period looking towards Esplanade Station and the town of Ryde — the signal box, scissors crossover and distortion of the conductor rail on the electric tramway are all worthy of note. The structure on the west side of the pier is the headquarters of the local rowing club; at one time, a life-boat was also stationed there. *R. A. Silsbury Collection*

With the ballroom having been long demolished, it is impossible to exactly recapture the older view; however, the roof of the Trinity House Pilot Station provided me with a very acceptable alternative on 9 March 1991. Only the piles to the right of the pier show where the rowing club once was, whilst to the left of the roadway, the tramway lies derelict and the signal box, pointwork and signal gantry have all gone — caught up in the progress that has seen electric motive power replace that of steam.

This 1950s aerial view of the pier, with Esplanade Station at the landward end, provides a plethora of detail - from a rarely seen angle. A Ventnor train is in the process of pulling away from No 1 platform; No 2 platform is also occupied. The vessels alongside are British Railways PS *Sandown*, MVs *Shanklin* and *Brading*, and the MV *Vecta* of Red Funnel Line. Note the ballroom and the extensive premises of the rowing club, together with the large number of passengers waiting to board the *Brading*. *IWSR Collection*

On 24 July 1990, not as busy as on the day of the 1950s photograph, movement is still evidenced by the arrival of the catamaran and the train waiting to move her passengers away. Note, beneath the water, the piles once supporting the rowing club and, next to Esplanade Station, the reclaimed land at the 'Hoverport'. *Hampshire Constabulary Air Support Unit*

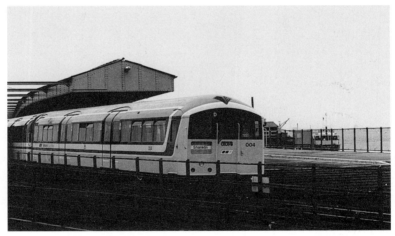

Two Adams '02' tank engines, the nearer being *Ningwood*, stand quietly at Pierhead Station on 10 July 1965, with the entrance to Portsmouth Harbour just discernible in the distance — from whence the first regular sailings to the Island are documented as far back as 1796. The stretch of track from Pierhead to St John's Road was originally operated under the joint auspices of the London, Brighton & South Coast and the London & South Western railways as a logical extension of their services to the South Coast from London and the suburbs. Note the bell: differences of opinion exist as to whether it was used to signal train departures or boat arrivals. *IWSR Collection*

When the Isle of Wight railway system — or, at least, its truncated remains — was electrified during the winter months of 1966/67, the opportunity was also taken to carry our major alterations at the Pierhead Station, the most obvious change being the reduction in the number of platforms from four to three. Here we see Class '483' No 004 about to depart from Platform 1 — once Platform 4 — with the 17.22 service to Shanklin on 13 June 1990.

The scene in 1927 — the last year in which the tram cars had open cabs and obtained their
motive power from a third-rail supply. From this year onwards, and until closure in 1969,
Drewry petrol-engined units worked the tramway. In the background a four-coach train, with
parcels van to the rear, stands waiting for clearance to depart from No 1 platform. *IWSR
Collection*

A much changed scene on 13 June 1990. The tramway is no more, the signal box has gone,
no semaphore signals remain and the ballroom has been demolished. However, the tramway
railings are the same, together with the wooden planking on the pier road.

Ryde Esplanade

Opened: 5 April 1880   OS Map Reference: SZ 594928

The Pier, Ryde, I.W.

A postcard view of the whole of the pier complex, with a southbound Adams '02' about to depart, and three fascinating road vehicles in the foreground. The card is dated 7 August 1931, but the view is of an earlier decade — for a signal box once stood where the open shelter at the platform end is now standing, and this was taken out of service in 1923. *R. A. Silsbury Collection*

Taken, as was the earlier shot, from the roof of the Esplanade Hotel, the 13 June 1990 view highlights many of the changes that have taken place as the century has progressed. Although the station building chimneys have been dismantled, the main roof is very little changed — and behind the down platform the bollards on the wharf still stand.

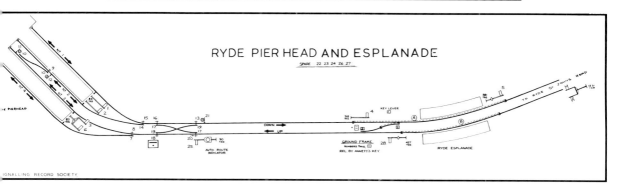

RYDE PIER HEAD AND ESPLANADE

SPARE 22 23 24 26 27

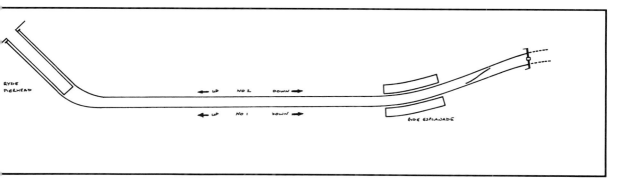

Osborne approaches Ryde Tunnel — 391 yards (c357 metres) long — with a well laden train for Ventnor during the summer of 1951. The tunnel lies below sea level and is prone to flooding. Road vehicle enthusiasts will admire the line-up of charabancs in the car park. *IWSR Collection*

Modern by Island standards, the latest ex-London Transport units in use were built in 1938! Here Class '483' Unit 002 accelerates into the tunnel on 13 June 1990, past what we now call luxury coaches. The size of the train may have shrunk, but the road coaches have certainly grown! Note the superstructure of the hovercraft just visible next to the footbridge — another modern touch.

The north portal of the Ryde Esplanade tunnel in June 1961; despite having twin arches at both ends, it is a single-arch, 'cut and cover' structure. Although the connection between St John's Road and Esplanade was made in the summer of 1880, the plaque below the railings bears the date 1881. The building on the right is the tunnel pumping station, provided to keep disruption from flood water to a minimum — and note the check rails provided on the tight curve out of the tunnel mouth. *P. Paye*

On 2 July 1990 the louvred windows have been bricked up, but the pumping station still carries out its same function — although raising of the trackbed during electrification has markedly reduced the incidence of flooding. Despite the change from steam to electric traction, it will be noted that the check rails are still a requirement.

Ryde St John's Road

Opened: 23 August 1864   OS Map Reference: SZ 596919

Looking to the north in the 1960s, with a Southern Vectis double decker crossing the St John's Road overbridge. Ryde Works, on the right (see pages 31-2), date from the 1870s and were modernised to the state shown in this view in 1938. *IWSR Collection*

On 2 July 1990, the awning on the down platform has been shortened, but still retains the smart IWR cast iron supports, and the Works have received a major update just two years before. The new building on the up platform is a rest room used by today's locomotive staff. Ryde St John's Road box is now the focal point for all signalling on the 'Island Line', control being centralised here when Sandown box was taken out of service in October 1988.

Ticket issued on 29 May 1963. *IWSR Museum Archives*

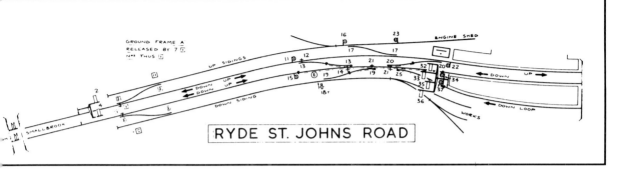

RYDE ST. JOHNS ROAD

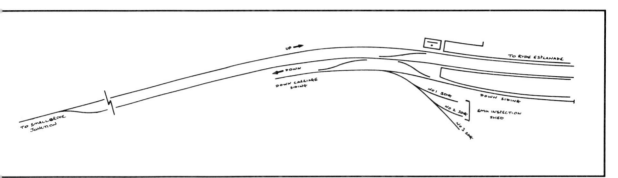

Merstone pulls into the up platform with a train from Cowes in the early 1930s. The importance of Ryde St John's Road to the Island railway system can be gauged from the number of different types of rolling-stock in the vicinity. The signal box, which once had its door at the other end, was moved to the Island in 1928 from Waterloo Junction. Note that two of the semaphore arms have been removed from the signal gantry, indicating a busy time of the year and that Smallbrook Box is 'switched in'. In the summer, the route to Smallbrook Junction was run as double track, and in the quieter months as two single lines. *IWSR Collection*

The 15.51 service from Shanklin pulls in past the same signal box some 50 or more years later on 2 July 1990. Note the gradient post on the up platform and the unchanged housing estate to the south. The land behind the platform has been sold out of railway ownership and is now a merchant's yard.

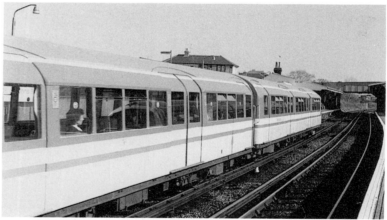

Ashey rumbles through the station on the morning of 5 September 1964, approaching St John's Road overbridge, with the 10.45 goods from Newport. Taken from the southern end of the down platform, this view gives a good impression of the size of the sheds, clearly visible beyond the station nameboard — with another, unidentified, Adams 'O2' standing on shed. Note the particularly tall signal beyond the bridge, with co-acting semaphore arms for ease of viewing from different distances. *K. Jagger*

The 09.11 Shanklin to Ryde Pierhead passenger service, operated by Class '483' Unit 006, provides us with a nice comparison shot some 27 years later on 24 March 1991. To the left, of course, Ryde sheds — the Mecca of many a trainspotting youngster in years gone by — have been demolished, but little else has been changed in the station itself and memories of steam days are easily evoked. The building beyond the station, denuded of many of its chimneys, is now in use as a Health Club.

Ryde Works

OS Map Reference: SZ 596919

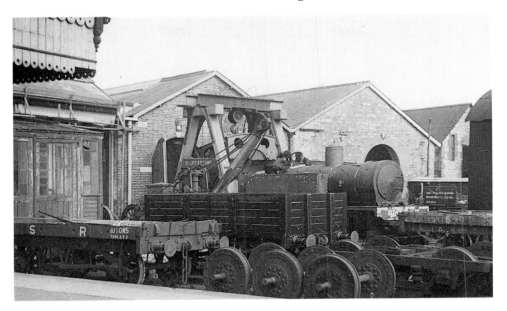

An interesting view of the Works yard, taken in the inter-war period, with an unidentified '02' receiving a complete major overhaul beneath the 25-ton hoist. Taken in the early 1930s, contrast the ramshackle appearance of the doors in this view with the smarter folding doors in the post-1938 view of St Johns Road station on page 26. *IWSR Collection*

A Class '483' car, once bearing the LRT designation '10255', stands at the Works entrance on 2 July 1990, having just come out from routine servicing. The track was raised during major upgrading works in 1988 to permit easy access to the underfloor traction motors on the '483' units.

The new Ryde Shed (up side): 'Beyer Peacock' *Wroxall* and Adams '02' *Sandown* stand above the maintenance pits, with cold fireboxes but no work being carried out on either loco. The overhead steel girders and crossmembers exemplify the Island tradition of seeming to use second-hand materials whenever possible: these items began their railway lives in the southern suburbs of London as part of the LB&SCR overhead electrification scheme. *Real Photographs/Ian Allan Ltd*

The refurbished Works (down side): The modern Works, looking out to the south on 2 July 1990, with second-hand equipment again prominent; ex-LRT stock Class '483' Unit 006, built in 1938, stands on the elevated service track and type '485/486' unit 485041, of 1923 to 1934 vintage, stands nearby above the inspection pit.

Smallbrook Junction

IWSR/BR Interchange Station opened: 21 July 1991
OS Map Reference: SZ 598905

Seen from near the 20-lever signal box, the double track curves in under Smallbrook overbridge from Ryde. Just visible is a semaphore signal (Ryde St John's up distant) mounted on the brick-work of the bridge, while members of the permanent way gang work near the down track. The heavy work of track relaying is about to begin. *IWSR Collection*

By coincidence the permanent way engineers were working on this stretch of the line again during my visit on 2 July 1990, with 'high visibility' vests now being mandatory wear; note the PW truck parked by the bridge. The unburnished rails in the foreground, not present in the days of steam, lead to a sand drag, into which Ryde box could switch any train that ran away approaching the stretch of single line leading on to Brading.

Salt in the wound — running past lengths of conductor rail already deposited between the up and down lines, *Fishbourne* approaches Smallbrook bridge in the summer of 1966 with a permanent way train carrying 'third rail' sections for the electrification programme — soon to bring the Adams '02' locomotive's proud career to an end! Concrete and sleeper-built fogmen's huts stand on either side of the track, the latter awaiting demolition. *T. P. Cooper*

Carrying the wrong destination indicator whilst *en route* to Ryde Pierhead, 'Island Line' series '483' Unit 005 passes a colour light signal at the same spot a quarter of a century later on 2 July 1990. The sleeper-built hut has disappeared, but the concrete structure is still in situ — and note the same broken notice in front of it!

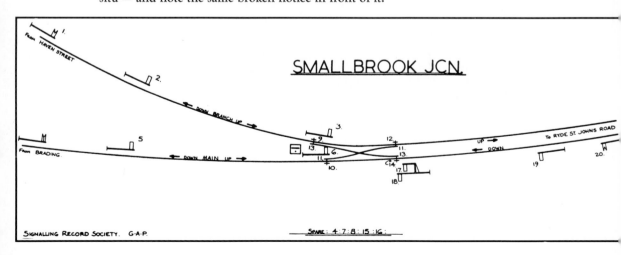

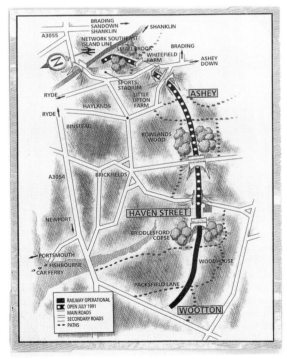

Smallbrook Junction is the target of the Isle of Wight Steam Railway's 1991 extension. *IWSR*

Brading hauls the six-coach 10.20 am service from Ryde Pierhead to Ventnor past the junction of the line to Newport on 15 August 1962. This photograph was actually taken from the bottom step of the stairs leading to Smallbrook signal box - a remote and secluded spot, with no direct road access and only the wildlife for company when trains were not passing. In the summer months, though, it was rare that the signalman would have had the luxury of time to admire the scenery around him! (The box was 'switched out' during the quiet winter months, and the up and down lines to St John's Road operated as two parallel single tracks - see page 28.)

Opened on 20 July 1991, Smallbrook Junction Station is now the interchange for the Isle of Wight Steam Railway and Island Line electric services, but is only open when the IWSR is operating. Between the two platforms the foundations of the Smallbrook Junction signal box can still be seen.

Brading

Opened: 23 August 1864   OS Map Reference: SZ 609868

The sharpness of the curve on which the station was built is very obvious in this fine view looking up towards Smallbrook Junction and, eventually, Ryde. Because Brading signal box, in the background, was so remote from the track, it was necessary for a 'runner' to be provided on busy days for single line token exchanges. Note the very fine ironwork of the canopy supports on the island platform, the footbridge also being a fine example of Victorian craftsmanship. *P. J. Relf*

Although the line has been singled, and the island platform and signal box taken out of use, the basic view on 13 June 1990 has changed little over the years. The main station building has been converted into a Community and Heritage Centre, and plans are afoot for the IWSR to acquire the signal box.

Cast iron IWR monogram built into the canopy supports, photographed on 13 June 1990.

Osborne was scrapped in 1955 in the first batch of Island '02s' to be withdrawn from service. The driver hurries to remount his steed in this classic 1932 shot, which also shows to good advantage the Westinghouse compressed air brake apparatus. Note also the prototype built-up coal bunker, first fitted experimentally to *Osborne* and later modified to become the Island standard. *A. R. Sedgwick Collection*

The former down line has been lifted, so 485043, at the head of the units forming the 10.22 ex-Ryde Pierhead on 13 June 1990, is not in an identical position in this comparison shot. The smart station lamps, giving off a gaslight effect, are actually powered by electricity. The house in the background is also of particular interest; above the door is an inset 'IWR 1877' monogram. Once the Station Master's residence, it later passed to the holder of the BR post of IOW Area Inspector and, on disestablishment in 1966, the last holder of the post, Mr Ron Russell, bought it for his own use.

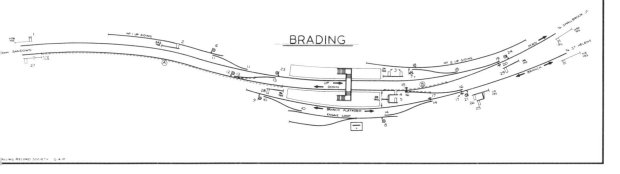

BRADING

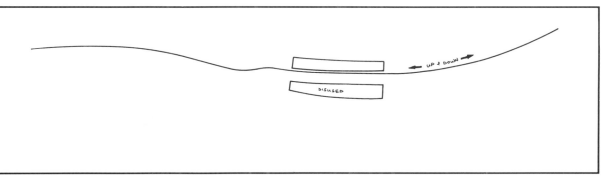

DISUSED

UP & DOWN

Looking in the opposite direction, *Brading* pulls a Ventnor to Ryde train through her 'home' station on 28 August 1965, with the token for the section to Smallbrook about to be collected by the train crew. There is, of course, no token on the footplate for exchange, the metals southwards to Sandown being double track. *L. Elsey*

There are currently eight Class '483' units in service with 'Island Line', with the final ninth unit due for delivery early in the summer of 1991. The unit here on 14 March 1991, with Driver Ron Wyatt at the controls, carries the designator '004' at the up end; however, '003' appears at the down end for, following almost simultaneous failures of the opposite ends of both units, the Ryde Works staff have carried out the unusual task of joining together the serviceable portions to enable full services to continue.

41

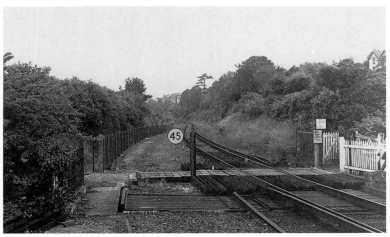

The view from the down platform looking towards Sandown, with rolling-stock stored in Chalk Siding. The unfenced footpath immediately adjacent to the down line led from Yarbridge, some ¼ mile south of this point, and provided direct access to the down platform or, via the crossing, to the small town of Brading. *IWSR Collection*

The footpath still crosses the line on 13 June 1990, but many of the fine railway artefacts have been removed. The '45' speed limit sign is very evident; this is the maximum speed permitted on Island metals, 5 mph higher than officially allowed in the days of steam. Note the pine tree still flourishing on the bank above the site of Chalk Siding.

Headed by *Ashey*, and carrying but a handful of passengers, a two-coach train moves off from the outer face of the island platform, used exclusively by traffic on the branch line to Bembridge. The buildings in the distance, to the left of the engine's smoke plume, are part of the local cement factory complex. *Pamlin Prints*

By 13 June 1990 the branch rails and those of the down main line have been lifted, and the signal gantry has been removed, but note the plinth of the gantry which can still be picked out beyond the platform slope. Its services no longer required, the cement factory has long been closed and its buildings razed to the ground.

St Helens

Opened: 27 May 1882
Closed: 21 September 1953

OS Map References:
Station: SZ 628886
Quay: SZ 631886

The only intermediate station on the line down to Bembridge from Brading, St Helens was an imposing structure, with the tall Tudor chimneys and elegant dormers being particularly pleasing to the eye. Of interest beyond the platform slope is the water column used to supply engines working the Quayside yard, and in the far distance the loading gauge, crossing gates to the Quay and the water tower beside the diminutive loco shed. This photograph was taken either at the time of the withdrawal of passenger services, or very shortly thereafter. *Pamlin Prints*

One of the most attractive station conversions that I have ever seen now graces the site. The awning is still in position and has been cleverly incorporated into a sun lounge along the whole platform length, whilst a first floor extension, above the old toilet block, has been blended in with equal skill. The gasometer, and buildings beyond it, have long since been razed to the ground.

The main commercial docks for the island until Medina Wharf was rebuilt in 1928, the provision of a manual crane and four rail-mounted steam cranes indicates just how busy the harbour was in its heyday. The coasters of Chaplin's shipping line, two seen lying here alongside the North Quay, were the prime carriers into St Helens from the mainland, their parent company holding the main LSWR transhipment contract. Note, also, the steam dredger fitted on a dumb barge (silting-up has always been a major problem), and the large buildings of the Gas Works in the middle distance. *Real Photographs/Ian Allan Ltd*

Today the emphasis has moved from commerce to pleasure, but the port is still very active. On 9 May 1990 new harbourside housing faces out over the water, the quay having been retitled 'Bembridge Marina'.

Used first in pre-Grouping days to stable the branch's saddle tank *Bembridge,* this view of the loco shed was taken post-1921 when it had been transferred to the care of the Permanent Way Department for use as a general store. The water tank was not part of the original structure, but was added some time between 1882 and 1889. *F. Brock/IWSR Collection*

On 9 May 1990 only the wall on the north side remained, together with the upright of one door frame — still with the same two large bolts in position! The road in the foreground leads to a yachting-orientated housing complex.

Bembridge

Opened: 27 May 1882   OS Map Reference: SZ 643886
Closed: 21 September 1953

Summer 1949, and an unidentified Adams '02' pulls its three-coach train into the single platform, past the coal siding, after the 2¾-mile run from Brading. A tiny turntable at the western end of the station — of only 16 ft 5 in diameter — was used as a sector plate to release locomotives not fitted for push-pull working before the return trip to the junction of the branch with the main Ryde to Ventnor line. Note, in the hazy distance, the high ground of Bembridge Down. *IWSR Collection*

The scene on 9 May 1990 has changed beyond recognition. The houses of Harbour Strand now stand on the site of the platform, the gap between the two longer terraces being almost exactly where the waiting passengers are sitting in the earlier photograph.

Fishbourne stands ready to depart with the branch line service back to St Helens and Brading on the afternoon of 16 September 1953, with closure now less than a week away. The open wagons in the siding, together with the coach behind the guard's van, would have been in use by the permanent way team, for little 'true' goods traffic came this far down the line in the 1950s. Note the 'scotch block' positioned in the siding to protect against the runaway of stored wagons. *J. H. Aston*

As we have seen, the houses of Harbour Strand, and their small yards, cover the spot where the station building and attendant trackbed were once so prominent. Note, however, as a link with the past, the toilet block on the right still in use on 9 May 1990, and the continuing lush growth of trees.

Fishbourne again, looking very spick and span on 29 March 1948, with an equally shiny set of push-pull-fitted twin bogie ex-LB&SCR coaches bringing up the rear. The large building behind the station was the Royal Spithead Hotel, now demolished. Note the ex-army haversack left on the platform seat at the extreme left, typical of 'war surplus' equipment put to civilian use in these early post-war years. *J. H. Aston*

No signs whatsoever of this corner of the Island's railway heritage are evident from the same angle on 9 May 1990, and what a contrast in building styles! I wonder if the flat roofs of today's buildings are as serviceable as those of the Victorian era?

Sandown

Opened: 23 August 1864   OS Map Reference: SZ 593845

Back on the main line, the next station towards Ventnor is Sandown, seen here in the summer of 1964 — with 'all eyes on the photographer' from the waiting passengers on the up island platform. The excellent view from the signal box located high overhead can be much appreciated. Until 1920, the IOWR had its headquarters within the station buildings on platform 1, and until 1956 trains to Newport set off and arrived at the outer face of the island platform (then platform 3). Note the small sign below the running-in board advising travellers that Sandown was also the station for Lake — which is no longer the case. *P. J. Relf*

Double track still runs through Sandown on 12 June 1990, but only to perform the function of a passing loop. The island platform buildings have gone, together with the signal box — the latter was demolished on 18 February 1989, but only after the 19th-century Saxby & Farmer lever frame had been removed and generously donated to the IWSR.

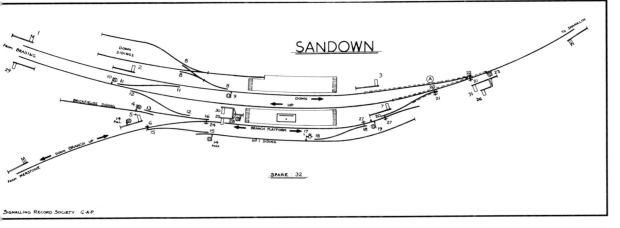

SANDOWN

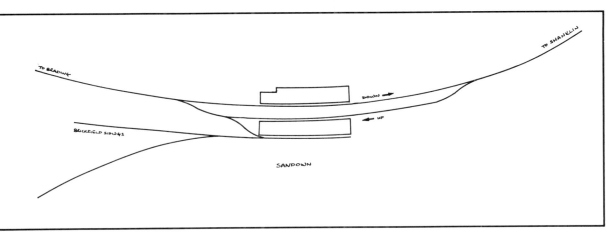

Sandown looking south just after Nationalisation, with lower quadrant signals still in use and three open wagons, used for sugar beet traffic, standing in the No 1 siding beyond the branch platform. The water tower next to the wagons was used by the Newport branch loco. I wonder what is attracting the attention of the waiting passengers below the concrete station nameboard? *IWSR Collection*

I took the comparison shot on 12 June 1990 about 40 yards further back along the platform in order to show, in the foreground, the roofing (with reinforced glass blocks) of the subway between the platforms. Beyond, note the many fascinating changes: the semaphore signals replaced by colour lights; the allotments in the background returned to meadow; the different lampshades, station nameboard and fencing; the '03' diesel standing where trains once stood at the branch platform; and, of course, the third rail. The gradient post on the left, however, still retains its same spot in a changing world!

The station entrance before the First World War, with horse-drawn carriages waiting for their next passengers. The nearer carriage appears to be what we would now call the 'courtesy bus' for the Sandown Hotel. The removal firm White & Co Ltd is still a thriving concern, with branches all over the British Isles. *IWSR Collection*

Essentially the same on 12 June 1990, only minor differences to the station building's façade are apparent, although BR's policy of raising capital by selling off surplus land has altered the overall scene somewhat in the nearby yard! Island Line Ltd's administrative offices now occupy the building's first floor.

Lake

IWR Station:
Opened: 1889
Closed: c1914
BR Station:
Opened: 9 July 1987

OS Map Reference: SZ 588827

OS Map Reference: SZ 590833

Midway between Lake Girder Bridge and Skew Bridge, Adams '02' *Brading* heads a six coach ex-Ryde Pierhead train along the single track towards Ventnor, on a pleasant Saturday afternoon in August 1966. Nearby was once the site of the County Cricket Ground, and it was to serve this that the original station at Lake was built. *T. P. Cooper*

Today's Lake station, serving the expanding residential area between the major resorts of Sandown and Shanklin, stands at this very spot. Jointly financed by British Rail and the Isle of Wight County Council, the facility has proved very popular with Islanders and visitors alike, and its future seems assured. Having dropped off its passengers — or 'customers' as BR now insists on calling them — Class '483' Unit 006 draws away towards Shanklin with the 09.42 Sunday service from Ryde Pierhead on 24 March 1991.

Shanklin

Opened: 23 August 1864   OS Map Reference: SZ 581819

Deep shadows, shorts, sunglasses and shirt-sleeves give the air of a typically English summer day to this undated post-war view of the station, looking from the up platform — which was not part of the original 'build', but was added when the line to Ventnor was opened in 1866. Note the elevated signal box, visible over the platform canopy. *P. J. Relf*

Having to be taken from a few yards north of the earlier photograph, because of the removal of the Landguard Road overbridge, this view shows to good effect the changes brought about by electrification and, subsequently, the bridge removal and the lifting of the up rails. As a thoughtful joint venture between BR and the local community, the site of the partly demolished up platform of the new terminus station has been turned into an attractive flower bed. The replacement tiles on the station building roof have mellowed with time, but are still quite obvious on 12 June 1990.

On the penultimate day of main-line steam operations on the Isle of Wight, *Seaview* shows a good head of steam as she pulls away from Shanklin bunker-first with a Ventnor to Ryde Pierhead train. Note the third rail conductors already in position, together with an assortment of engineering paraphernalia at the trackside. *B. Stephenson/IWSR Collection*

With the electric service now a well established part of Island life, ex-LRT Series '483' Unit 007 accelerates away with the 10.11 service up to Ryde on 12 June 1990, passing the same location — but on the old down line. The extension of the single platform left in use is quite obvious in this view; however, the house on the right with the attractive bargeboarding is almost completely obscured by the fresh growth of foliage.

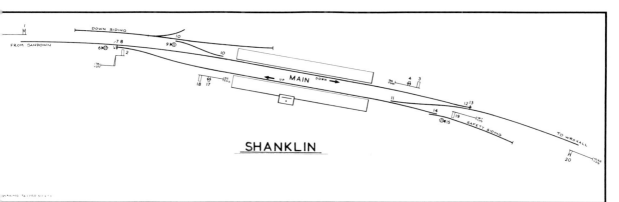

SHANKLIN

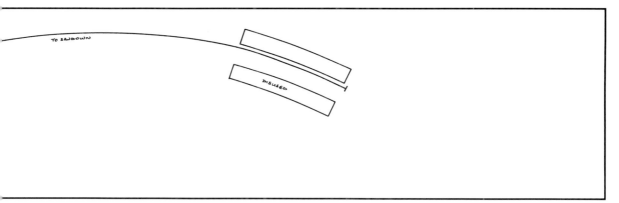

A fine line-up of private cars and taxis on the station concourse on 20 May 1956. By this date, of course, the offer (on the nameboard above the entrance to the booking hall) of 'Cheap Tickets Daily To All Parts Of The Island' no longer held true; the lines to Ventnor West, Bembridge, Freshwater and Newport, via Sandown, were now all closed to traffic! *A. E. Bennett*

A full complement of taxis stands outside the station entrance on 14 March 1991 but, in fact, no trains were operating and all services down from Ryde were terminating at Lake, with a bus connection being provided between Sandown and Shanklin for through passengers. The closure was due to track gradient alterations, and accompanying platform raising, following a train runaway earlier in the year.

Apse Bank
between Shanklin and Wroxall

OS Map References: Upper Hyde Lane Bridge: SZ 576817
Cliff Bridge: SZ 568814
Three Arch Bridge: SZ 557814

In the colours and markings of British Railways, *Shanklin* runs below the centre span of Three Arch Bridge, with the gentle curve of Apse Bank around St Martin's Down lying ahead. The bank, named after the nearby Apse Manor, is generally considered to be the stretch of track lying between Shanklin and Wroxall, although the long climb actually starts from near the site of the present Lake Station and doesn't end until Ventnor Tunnel is entered. Although the climb up the bank called for the best from both locomotive and crew, the trip back to Shanklin was a more relaxed affair, with a chance to enjoy the scenery — and even to stop, so the story goes, for the odd spot of illicit mushroom picking! *A. E. Bennett*

The trackbed on 10 March 1991 with Three Arch Bridge — although masked by much more undergrowth than would have been allowed in railway days — still dominating the skyline. In its old age it has taken on a new lease of life; local climbing enthusiasts enjoy scaling its well-preserved brickwork! The trackbed itself now forms a footpath from Wroxall to Shanklin.

Wroxall

Opened: 15 September 1866
Closed: 17 April 1966

OS Map Reference:
SZ 552799

An early spring evening in 1964, and *Brading* prepares to move off up the continuing incline towards Ventnor Tunnel. Little over two years before final closure, the up siding beyond Castle Road bridge is still in use by goods traffic. *IWSR Collection*

By 10 June 1990 the footbridge, vantage point for so many evocative photographs over the years, has gone — as have the platforms and the bungalow-like station building. However, the old bacon factory's upper floor and roof still dominate the skyline, but now overlook a light industrial park.

Nearer the end of the up platform, we are looking towards Shanklin, via Apse Bank, with the gradient marker at the rear of the down platform emphasising the relative severity of the long climb towards Ventnor Tunnel. *IWSR Collection*

The ivy has been removed from the walls of the old hotel on the left and washing lines have usurped trolleys, carts and milk churns on 10 June 1990. Since the closure of the line, through traffic over Castle Road Bridge — as well as below it — has ceased, all vehicles now routeing around the new industrial estate.

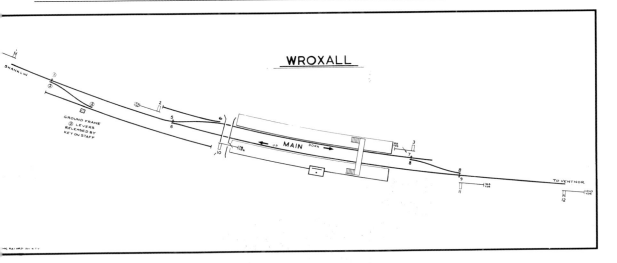

WROXALL

SHANKLIN

GROUND FRAME
② LEVERS
RELEASED BY
KEY ON STAFF

MAIN

UP   DOWN

TO VENTNOR

Looking towards St Boniface Down and Ventnor, the Station Hotel and the single storey station building are on the right; thirsty travellers could gain access to and from the platform via a door to the Public Bar! Beyond the points at the end of the down loop, the signal has already been pulled off to allow the next up train from Ventnor entry off the single line section into the station. *A. R. Sedgwick*

The Station Hotel has been turned into housing units, but all other signs of the railway have been erased by 10 June 1990. Beautiful St Boniface Down, with its fantastic views back over the Island and out over the English Channel, remains unaltered by the passage of time — save for a new radio mast at the forward relay station of the London Air Traffic Control Centre.

Ventnor Tunnel

OS Map References: North Portal: SZ 558793
South Portal: SZ 561780

Showing a good head of steam, *Shorwell* plunges into the northern end of the 1,312 yards (c1,200 metres) of Ventnor Tunnel, with the regulator about to be eased as the gradient changes to a downhill slope all the way to the Ventnor platforms. Assumed high maintenance costs on the tunnel were one of the main reasons for the closure of this commercial lifeline to the Island's sunniest resort. *R. A. Silsbury Collection*

The heavy growth on the trackside banks precluded today's picture being taken from quite the same spot — but on 10 June 1990 the sad change to this once vibrant spot is there for all to see! Firmly secured against all visitors — the bolder local teenagers loved the tunnel as an adventure playground before the gates were installed — the tunnel is now maintained by Southern Water for, in addition to the water main using the bore, spring water — which gave the builders major problems when the tunnel was being cut — is also taken out. Can the decision to close the tunnel to rail traffic, and cut off the resort of Ventnor from the rest of BR's network, ever be really justified?

Ventnor

Opened: 15 September 1866
Closed: 17 April 1966

OS Map Reference:
SZ 561778

The south end of the tunnel in 1950 and, having arrived earlier at No 1 platform, *Osborne* runs around the island platform to the front of the train ready for a bunker-first departure. Note the small covered way at the front of the signal box, built to allow the transfer of the single line tokens between enginemen and signalmen without the latter needing to go down to ground level — or out in the wet! Of particular interest at the station was a portable gangway, used to provide access to the island platform by being placed over No 1 road in the right foreground when traffic density required the use of its outer face. A bellpush was provided to request permission from Ventnor signal box to place the gangway in position and, again, to advise when the obstruction was removed. *Dr P. T. Moore*

The Ford P100 pick-up truck stands almost exactly where *Osborne* did 40 years before, but on 9 May 1990 the coal yard is now home to the industrial units of the aptly named 'Old Station Industrial Estate'.

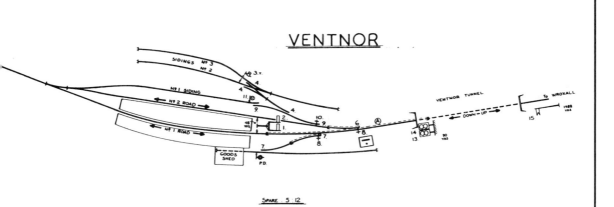

VENTNOR

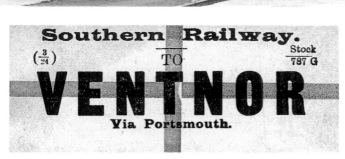

IWSR Collection

A fascinating early morning view from the slopes of St Boniface Down. Coal wagons stand outside the caves used by local fuel and builders' merchants as stores, the main platform is a hive of activity, and an unidentified Adams '02' tank waits for the last coach doors to be closed before moving off on the 12½-mile journey back to Ryde Pierhead. *IWSR Collection*

From the same position on 9 May 1990, only the cave entrances and the station hotel provide a link with the past, for the whole site has been taken over by light industry. Here, as elsewhere on the Island, the motor car can be seen to rule supreme.

An aged but nevertheless extremely interesting photograph of the caves during IWR days — the company's markings are just visible on the sides of the open coal wagons. Island railways always carried vast amounts of coal traffic, both for their own use and for domestic consumption, and here we see railway stocks in the foreground, with sacks for distribution to private customers standing beyond. *R. A. Silsbury Collection*

In common with every other railway artefact within the station yard, the ground outside the caves no longer bears witness to a fascinating history. Today the caves have ceased to be used by local coal merchants, but, as the photograph shows, they are still found useful by building contractors and those plying allied trades.

Part 2

Cowes to Newport and Ashey

Cowes

Opened: 16 June 1882
Closed: 21 February 1966

OS Map Reference:
SZ 496960

Standing at the junction of Terminus Road and Carvel Lane, Cowes station maintained basically the same exterior facade from its being extended in 1891 until its final days of service. It is seen here in May 1965. The main entrance to the glass-roofed concourse was via the wooden steps to the right of the building, although a level entrance was also available a little further up Terminus Road for those of limited agility. The station, well known for its excellent floral displays, was busy enough to boast a W. H. Smith's bookstall during the tourist season. *T. P. Cooper*

Only the two pavements in the foreground remain to link this photograph with that from the railway era. The Portsea Island Co Op store now occupies the site of the station building, while former railway land to its left is now the main Cowes bus stop. On the late afternoon of 28 March 1996, Southern Vectis bus service 1A pulls away towards Sandown, via Newport - a journey that could once have been made by rail!

The view of the station from Granville Road Bridge, with token exchange being carried out between one of the footplatemen on the '02' and the signalman. Coaching stock was kept made up in semi-permanent sets, hence the designator figures '488' on the rear coach of the rake standing at Platform 3, adjacent to which stand a brake van and a laden open wagon. The attractive iron footbridge did not, as might be expected, join the platforms to each other; it maintained public access between Terminus Road and Cross Street, which had been severed when the station was rebuilt in 1891. Beyond it, note the unusual layout of the Roman Catholic Church in the background — chimneys on one end and the cross on the other. The church and the priest's accommodation are both under the one roof! *P. J. Relf*

After years of indecision about the use of the site, and the adjacent Denmark Road School site, redevelopment is in full swing — with many of the old houses adjacent to the station also having been demolished. Even the Granville Road Bridge itself is no more, although the new road replacing it still bears that title. At ground level, next to the grass turfs, the site of the signal box and the old coal bay can still be distinguished. (The station running-in board, seen next to the box, now stands in a private Cowes garden.)

($\frac{2}{46}$) **SOUTHERN RAILWAY.**

(787 L.A.)

FROM WATERLOO TO

COWES

Via PORTSMOUTH & RYDE.

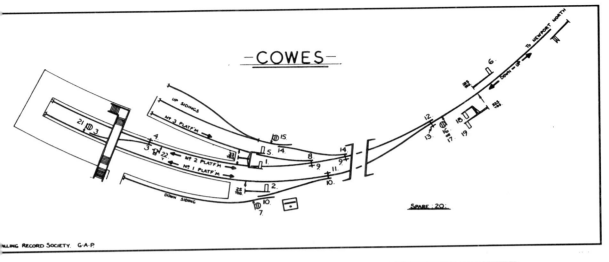

Cowes to Cement Mills — a Southern Railway Cheap Day ticket issued in the BR era (old stock!) on 19 February 1966. *IWSR Museum Archives*

Climbing the 1 in 145 gradient from the station towards Mill Hill Tunnel, *Shanklin* draws a Cowes to Ryde Pierhead train over St Mary's Road bridge on a fine summer's day in June 1965. Older Cowes residents knew this area as Binney Hill, its name before the road was lowered and extended under the railway. *T. P. Cooper*

As would be expected in the 1990s, there are now more cars in the street but, apart from the very obvious removal of the underbridge, St Mary's Road has changed remarkably little over the years. Even the raised 'mall' footpath on the left, a reminder of the days when the road was lowered, is still present.

Mill Hill

Opened: 16 June 1862
Closed: 21 February 1966

OS Map Reference:
SZ 497954

Emerging from the 208 yards (c190 metres) of Mill Hill Tunnel, the line entered the single-platform Mill Hill station serving the southern suburbs of Cowes, located on a sharp curve in the line less than half a mile from the town's terminus. There are no passengers present, but the station did enjoy two busy periods each weekday as numerous workmen made their way to or from the industrial sites in the Mill Hill area. *Pamlin Prints*

Although a lush ivy growth has attached itself to the tunnel brickwork, and new housing dominates the skyline, the view on 10 May 1990 is not difficult to reconcile with that of yesteryear. The Council has even provided a bench seat at the same spot as BR once did! In railway days, housing development over the line was not permitted because of the shallow cover over the tunnel arch; obviously modern methods have permitted building, for the tunnel itself remains in use as the local gun club's range.

The station in June 1950, with the entrance to Mill Hill Tunnel in the background. Note, beneath the gas lamp, the beautiful old weighing machine — but again not a passenger in sight! *A. R. Sedgwick*

The Council has filled in the trackbed and, beyond the Body Tech Unit, which fills most of the frame today, has built an attractive linear garden.

The unusual wooden awning following the slope of the roof is an attractive feature, the station being reminiscent of a Swiss chalet! The station exit was a footpath leading up the embankment on the right to the main road. *Pamlin Prints*

The sweep of the platform edge is still in evidence on 10 May 1990 but, looking up the line, all other signs of the station have been eliminated. The electrical transformer remains, but is now enclosed in wooden fencing. What a shame that its purpose today is not to power the third rail!

Smithards Lane Crossing

OS Map Reference: SZ 497952

Looking northwards down the line, through the short 20 mph speed restriction, towards Mill Hill station and Cowes. A solitary five-plank wagon stands in the single 'Gas House' siding, which also served the local coal merchant, whilst the crossing keeper (in 'part uniform') casts a suspicious eye past his residence towards the photographer. Because of the terms of the original running agreement, the gates beyond the house will remain closed against road traffic as usual. *K. Paye*

By 10 May 1990 the crossing keeper's cottage and the gas works have gone, and a very smart hall belonging to the local Scout Troop stands on the site of the former. Furthermore, motor traffic now has unimpeded passage down towards the industrialised banks of the River Medina!

RYDE ST JOHN'S ROAD: No 21 *Sandown*, with a five-coach down train, stands ready to pull away towards Smallbrook Junction on 19 June 1965. Note, above the up platform canopy and beyond the St John's Road over-bridge, the tall home signal - positioned so for ease of driver viewing. With freight traffic still on offer on the Island, open wagons and vans stand on the metals of No 1 and No 2 sidings.

With 'Shanklin' clearly displayed on its destination board, Class 483 unit No 004 eases away from St John's Road with the 15.04 service from Ryde Pierhead. The modernised works buildings, together with the shortening of the down platform canopy, show clearly in this March 1996 view. It is interesting to note that when the 'past' picture was taken, 004 had already been in service with London Underground for some 27 years! *C. L. Caddy/Colin Pomeroy*

RYDE SHED: Early on the evening of 10 September 1966 three of the hard-working Adams 'O2s', *Chale*, *Freshwater* and *Calbourne*, stand quietly on shed at Ryde. (To me there is as much pure railway atmosphere - call it nostalgia if you wish! - in this view as in one of, say, *Flying Scotsman* hard at work on the LNER's mainland metals.) At the adjacent Ryde St John's Road Station, both platforms are occupied by passing passenger trains.

Almost 30 years later, on 19 March 1996 and with most of the former railway land sold off, the only obvious links with the past are the ex-Waterloo Junction signal box and, to its right, the roofs of the works buildings beyond the down platform. Sadly the box is no longer trimmed in the memory-evoking green colours of the Southern Railway! *C. L. Caddy/Colin Pomeroy*

SANDOWN: Christmas Eve 1966, with the end of passenger steam operations just one week away, sees No 16 *Ventnor* awaiting the off from Sandown's down platform for the run southwards to its 'home town'. Sections of third rail, for the conclusion of the Island's electrification programme, can be seen stacked next to the old Newport branch platform; on the main line, however, these conductor rails have already been installed.

With only the stop at Lake ahead of it on the run down to Shanklin, unit No 004 stands ready to depart with the two-car 1.23 pm service from Ryde Pierhead. (Passengers who joined the connecting service from London Waterloo, which departed at 11.00, will be in Shanklin only some 2¾ hours after the commencement of their journey.) The reduction is size of the waiting room on the up platform, the size of the electrically powered train compared to its steam cousin, and the foreshortening of the canopy over the down platform can all be readily appreciated in this 19 March 1996 view. *C. L. Caddy/Colin Pomeroy*

LAKE: New Year's Eve 1966 was the last day of Island steam, and No 17 *Seaview* shows her paces as she hauls a train packed with rail enthusiasts up the gradient past the 7½ milepost (hidden by the loco) towards the uncontrolled foot crossing from the village of Lake to the nearby cliff-top gardens. In addition to the 'trespassing' photographer, note the shadows of the many other photographers in the foreground - recording this eventful day for posterity.

On 28 March 1996, having just pulled away from the second station to serve Lake - opened on 9 July 1987 and out of sight beyond the chain-link fence on the left - composite electric unit No 003/001 passes the same location almost 30 years later with the 12.42 pm service from Ryde Pierhead to Shanklin, having departed Lake on schedule at 1.03 pm. The land on the left of the line has been completely redeveloped, the house with the prominent dormer window being masked by modern housing, but Cliff Gardens remain as unspoilt as they ever were.
C. L. Caddy/Colin Pomeroy

WROXALL: On an August day in 1963, and with her driver finally able to ease the regulator after the climb up Apse Bank from Shanklin, an unidentified Adams 'O2' passes the village's bacon factory building on the approach to Wroxall Station. No doubt the holidaymakers occupying the seats in all five carriages will have been viewing the leaden sky with some trepidation, and hoping for better weather when they set out for the Ventnor beaches the next day!

Although the former trackbed is now the site of a light industrial unit, producing a range of electrical components, the old buildings to the north of the line have altered very little with the passage of time. Between the ivy growths on the lighter-coloured building can still be seen the pale green sign from the days when the bacon factory was in full production, while the structure of the former loading bay - once served by a trailing siding off the down passing loop - is still equally obvious to even the most casual of observers.

If plans proceed to reinstate the line between Shanklin and Ventnor, the currently preferred option at Wroxall is for the Teknacron Circuits factory to be relocated, the Castle Road bridge (from which the photographs were taken) to be demolished, a new station building to be erected on the opposite side of the track from its predecessor, and a cut-and-cover tunnel to be built below the current St Martins Road car park. *ISWR Collection/Colin Pomeroy*

COWES: Running bunker-first, and with the signalman returning to his box after the token exchange, an unidentified Adams 'O2' pulls a rake of four coaches out of Cowes Station, past Cowes box and towards Granville Road Bridge on a beautiful day in the mid-1960s. To the left of the signal arm can be seen the bulk storage yard of the local coal merchant, while at least one passenger coach stands idle in the up siding.

On 28 March 1996 only the house chimneys on the extreme right of the photograph and the small piece of rough ground adjacent to the satellite dish on the left remain of what one could have viewed from the bridge in the days of the railway. Everything else has gone, and the massive bulk of the apartments of Admiral Gardens now completely dominates the skyline. *IWSR Collection/Colin Pomeroy*

NEWPORT: On a beautiful summer day in July 1964 'O2' *Brading* departs Newport Station to follow the valley of the River Medina with a three-coach down service to Cowes, with Mill Hill Station the only scheduled stop *en route*. Note, standing in the down bay and sidings, a single box van and a rake of open wagons. The rails in the foreground no longer carry trains to the western end of the Island, the former Freshwater, Yarmouth & Newport Railway's line having been given up in the autumn of 1953.

It is hard to accept that the photograph taken on 28 March 1996 is from the same spot - or even from somewhere remotely adjacent - but I assure you that it is (although from a slightly lower elevation, due to contouring). The only links between the 'past' and 'present' scenes are the white chalk faces of Shide Chalk Pit and the headquarters of the Isle of Wight Council - home of England's first unitary authority. The cyclist is approaching the Newport bypass from the nearby industrial estate, the development of both of which has blotted out all signs of former railway existence for the first mile or so of the route to Cowes. Nearby, the Railway Medina Hotel, located at the entrance to the former station approach road, boasts a fine selection of old railway photographs, and is worth considering as a watering hole if you are in the area! *IWSR Collection/Colin Pomeroy*

ASHEY: Operating the 11.31 Cowes to Ryde Pierhead service on 11 September 1965, Adams 'O2' No 17 *Seaview* comes off the approach curve and over Gate House Lane crossing towards the original up platform - the down platform, as can be seen, had long since been taken out of use. The station house was at this time is a very sorry state - but ready for development!

Over 120 years since Ashey station first opened, the IWSR's 'O2' No W24 *Calbourne* with a three-coach train passes through on 28 March 1996, forming the 2.15 pm service from Havenstreet to Smallbrook Junction, on just the third day of steam for the summer season. The station is now operated as a halt on an 'on request' basis, but on this occasion passengers neither sought to alight nor board the train. *Hugh Ballantyne/Colin Pomeroy*

Medina Wharf

Wharf opened: 1877
Wharf closed: 1967

OS Map References:
Wharf: SZ 500944
Halt: SZ 499943

Located to the north of the pointwork leading into the Wharf yard, the diminutive gas-lit halt was used 'on request' by those who elected not to travel to work by foot or cycle, no road having been laid in those days. No shelter for passengers was ever provided. In the far distance the footbridge over the line, serving a public footpath leading from Somerton to the river bank, can be seen; today only the bridge uprights remain. *IWSR Collection*

At first glance, no signs at all of the halt are visible. However, a diligent search of the undergrowth on 29 June 1990 revealed three of the cut-down sleeper uprights still in position, together with some old rail used as fence stanchions.

Brading hauls the 12.30 Ryde Pierhead to Cowes train along the embankment above Medina Wharf on 9 August 1963. The steepness of the gradient from the yard up to the main line is quite obvious from this angle. *E. Wilmshurst*

The railway bank itself is still a prominent feature on the skyline and the unmade road still runs over the same ground. The tall pole carrying the floodlamp in the 1963 picture is still standing on 29 June 1990 but, apart from a discarded sleeper in the foreground, little else remains to tell of the railway's years in occupation.

The scene on 5 September 1964 down at wharfside level, looking north towards the transporter cranes and water tower, with the town of East Cowes just visible across the river in the hazy distance beyond the 'dumb' barge. As the loads in the five-plank open wagons in the sidings show, the main cargo into the Island via the wharf was coal — although it was also regularly used by the railway authorities for the shipment to and from the mainland of rolling-stock and locomotives. *K. Jagger*

Today's rolling-stock movements are normally carried out via 'Wightlink's' Portsmouth to Fishbourne car ferry service, but the wharf is still a constant scene of activity. With large silos dominating the scene on 26 September 1990, the coaster *City of Portsmouth* unloads her cargo of gravel — utilising a much smaller crane than was the norm in years gone by!

With the other small halt on the banks of the River Medina — Cement Mills — as the next possible stop *en route* to Newport, *Alverstone* draws away from Medina Wharf Halt on 3 September 1965. The points giving access to the Wharf are directly behind the photographer, whilst in the far distance stand industrial buildings on the outskirts of West Cowes. *A. E. Bennett*

With the trackside undergrowth no longer regularly cut back as a precaution against fire caused by sparks from passing locomotives, the scenery on both sides of the old line is now masked by lush greenery. However, the unmade road within the wharf area can just be seen, together with glimpses of the meadow to the west. On an overcast Sunday morning in March 1991, two cyclists retrace the steps of *Alverstone*, with a jogger and his dog in hot pursuit and a teenager searching the bushes to the right of the path for his missing ferret!

Cement Mills Halt

OS Map Reference: SZ 503917

A misty early autumn view — 5 September 1954 — looking northwards, with the rather primitive structure of the halt on the left and the entrance to the cement mills sidings off to the right of the track. The crossing road leads down to the riverside wharf, maritime access to which was strictly controlled by the state of the tide. This photograph is unusual in that it actually shows a waiting passenger on the wooden platform! After the works ceased to operate, Cement Mills Halt was removed from the timetable, but 'on request' stops were still made for fishermen and ornithologists using this corner of the Medina Valley. *K. Jagger*

Although superficially no railway remains can be seen from this angle today, a careful search on 26 September 1990 revealed a short length of unlifted rail lying between the roadway, now made up, and the left-hand post of the cycle path gates. Locally produced cement is no longer carried to and from here by train or boat, but the wharf continues to see a considerable amount of commercial shipping movements — as well as the passage of pleasure craft sailing to the Folly Inn moorings and as far up the River Medina as Newport Quay.

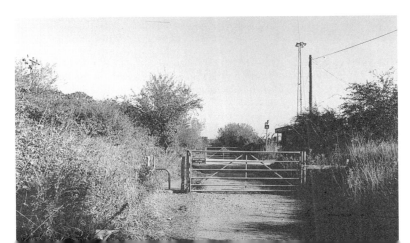

A fascinating 1909 view looking towards the sidings, with the line from Cowes curving away in the distance. Note how the flat-bottom rails are secured directly to the sleepers without the use of chairs, and that in IWCR days the platform had no slope at the end. *A. B. MacLeod/IWSR Collection*

The public right of way follows the curve of the lifted line to Cowes. A 'joggle' in the right-hand verge, next to the large bush, marks the entrance to the old siding; the storage tanks form part of the modern-day Esso fuel complex.

A fine panoramic view of the Cement Mills on 23 November 1909, looking down the untarmaced Stag Lane towards a sea of chimneys. The crossing gate is clearly visible and, to its left, the roof of the halt, whilst in the distance can be seen the masts of sailing barges tied alongside. *A. B. MacLeod/IWSR Collection*

On 7 May 1990 the hedge is no longer neatly 'laid', or even trimmed; the lady exercising her two dogs shows where the rails crossed the lane. All connections with cement have not, however, been severed, for Blue Circle still operates from the site and small coasters still grace the wharf.

Mill Pond Viaduct

OS Map Reference: SZ 503915

Cement Mills Halt and the old workings left behind, *Whitwell* eases over the viaduct with the 13.24 Cowes to Ryde Pierhead service on 29 July 1964. This nine-span bridge, built in 1875 to replace an earlier structure, had a 10 mph speed restriction on it right up to the withdrawal of services. *K. Paye*

The Mill Pond, and its immediate surroundings, are now a nature reserve. Because the viaduct now forms part of the Cowes to Newport foot and cycle path, extra fencing has been installed for safety reasons. The extra fencing is very obvious in this 7 May 1990 view, but the original metal guardrail is still readily visible on the far side of the public right of way as it curves down to path level. The telegraph pole is still in the same spot, but has had the attentions of a British Telecom maintenance team in the not too distant past!

Newport

IWCR Station:
Opened: 1 June 1879
Closed: 21 February 1966

OS Map Reference:
SZ 501895

In this general view of the north end of the station, taken in the 1930s when the Southern Railway held sway on the Island, *Bonchurch* is seen running 'light engine' along the main up line past the carriage cleaning depot. By now the upper storey of the station building, previously the domain of the IWCR Management, housed the offices of the 'Operating Assistant for the Isle of Wight'. *A. B. MacLeod*

Only the distinctive front wall of the old electricity works, just visible over the line of coaches on the extreme left of the earlier photograph, ties this 30 June 1990 picture with its counterpart. The new by-pass does not follow the exact line of the old Cowes to Newport trackbed, the equivalent railway orientation being from the left of the nearest lamp post to the right of a roundabout sign in the middle distance.

A fine view of the south end of Newport Station post-1956, the stop board and light being in position to preclude trains going, should there have been a signalling error, forward towards the redundant Sandown line (see Part 4) — although the drawbridge over the River Medina has yet to be removed and the rails lifted. To the right of the stock standing in the carriage siding can be seen part of the Newport shed complex, whilst in the distance stands the North signal box. *IWSR Collection*

Today all traces of the station platforms and buildings have gone, the Newport by-pass being routed through here. Taken at 6.30 in the morning, this 30 June 1990 scene gives no indication of the traffic build-up that will occur during the next couple of hours.

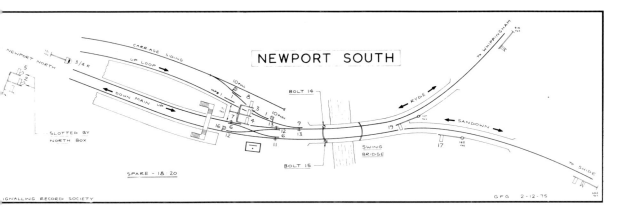

Ryde to Cowes via Newport — a ticket issued on 30 May 1963. *IWSR Museum Archives*

Whitwell observes the speed restriction on the viaduct over the River Medina as she runs in with the 1.40 pm Ryde to Newport goods train on the afternoon of 23 November 1965. Just discernable beyond the middle arch is the bastion for the long defunct low-level line connecting Newport Station with the commercial sidings once laid down along the eastern side of Newport Quay. *T. P. Cooper*

The bridge carrying the Newport by-pass follows virtually the same path across the river as its predecessor once did (it is actually displaced a few yards to the north-east); however, much else has changed — in addition to the shipping and state of the tide! The British Road Services Warehouse in the background has now been converted into luxury riverside accommodation, whilst on the opposite bank Sharp's Timber Yard has been replaced by a community centre. The trees in the distance, though, remain unchanged in this 29 June 1990 view.

The southern end of the short Newport Tunnel, 73 yards (c66.5 metres) long, which runs under the A3054 road joining the county town to Ryde, looms ahead as an unidentified Adams '02' hauls an early morning goods train along the single-line track out of Newport in August 1965. Note, on the bank to the left of the cutting, the 9¾ milepost. *T. P. Cooper*

Realigned to allow for recent road-building, the tunnel has been spared the fate of being sealed up for the rest of its days; it now allows the passage of pedestrians and cyclists below the roadway, as a point of interest and conversation on Public Footpath N175, leading out towards Fairlee.

Whippingham

Opened: 20 December 1875
Closed: 21 September 1953

OS Map Reference:
SZ 524915

Built to serve Queen Victoria's beloved Osborne House, 2½ miles away towards the mouth of the Medina Valley, the station was eventually made available to the local public. However, being so isolated — even today the only adjacent building is the Island Crematorium — passenger figures were always low. Here, an unidentified '02' pulls in with a three-coach up train to Ryde. *IWSR Collection*

Allowed to fall into disrepair when services were withdrawn, the station house has been lovingly restored into an attractive family home, but the tall wooden fence has had to be erected to maintain a modicum of privacy from passers-by on the public footpath.

When the station was built, the down platform was actually 9 feet longer than the up; this view shows well how much it was shortened by the Southern Railway after Grouping. The passing loop, installed in 1912, remained in use until 1956, three years after the station's closure on economic grounds — a foretaste of things to come in 1966 to the rest of the Cowes to Ryde line. *IWSR Collection*

Restored to its former glory — even the woodwork is painted to reflect the colours of the post-war years — modern garden furniture has now replaced the bench seats, baggage trolleys and oil lamps.

An extremely rare Whippingham ticket. *Courtesy of Andrew Britton*

WHIPPINGHAM

Wootton

IWCR Station:
Opened: 20 December 1875
Closed: 21 September 1953

OS Map Reference: SZ 535915

IWSR Station:
Opened: 31 May 1987

OS Map Reference: SZ 537913

Taken in June 1950, this view up the line through the Station Road overbridge and towards the single siding shows well the booking-office and waiting room located in one of the arches. Only just over ½ mile from the village centre, Wootton was more centrally located than the majority of the country stations on the Island and, until the advent of the motor bus, profited accordingly. The cause of the early closure of the station was the bank of constantly moving, water-laden clay opposite the platform. When Whippingham was removed from the timetable on economic grounds in September 1953, British Railways closed Wootton at the same time to reduce ongoing maintenance costs. *A. R. Sedgwick*

It is hard, today, to envisage the scene of 40 years ago, for all memories of the railway have been covered in a sea of slippery clay, dense undergrowth and towering trees. Beyond the road bridge, now back-filled in, stands the IWSR's new Wootton station.

A fine view of the platform, with the passenger access ramp leading up past the Station Master's house to the road. Note the small pegs protruding above the sleepers, used by the Permanent Way engineers to monitor any track creep caused by the movement of the clay. *J. H. Aston*

The station house still displays the IWCR logo but, of course, this 1 July 1990 view only ties in to the earlier one because the nameboard is the same! Here we see the IWSR's new station, built on the other side of the road bridge from its predecessor. The fine collection of preserved wagons parked in the engineers' siding brings an air of 'years gone by' to the present scene.

The IWSR's Brighton 0-6-0 'Terrier', IWC No 11, receives the single line token from the Wootton signalman before departing with the 12.20 pm service to Havenstreet on 1 July 1990.

The starter signal has been pulled 'off' from Wootton box and IWC No 11 eases out of the terminus with the 1.00 pm train on the same day. The box has had an interesting history: it started life with the FYNR at Newport and was moved to Freshwater in 1927, where it remained in use until that station's closure in 1953. It then was used as a bus shelter, returning to its original purpose at Wootton in 1987, but now equipped with an 8-lever frame — part of that from the old Shanklin box.

Havenstreet

Opened: 20 December 1875   OS Map Reference: SZ 555898
Closed: 21 February 1966
Re-opened: 1971

A view of Havenstreet station from the leading coach of an up train from Newport as it eases down the slope from Wootton before coming to a halt. The building to the right of the other train — destination Cowes — originally belonged to the Havenstreet Gasworks. Opened here in 1886, and served by a single siding, the works closed down in the 1920s. *IWSR Collection*

Deep in the midday shadows of 26 September 1990, one of the IWSR's hard-working diesels stands quietly in Goosefield Sidings next to the Works building, as a 'Terrier'-hauled service from Wootton draws past the signal gantry and up to the island platform. Even this late in the tourist season, a very respectable number of passengers are waiting to board the train for its next return journey.

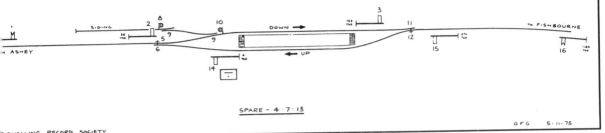

HAVEN STREET

SPARE - 4·7·13

G F G   5·11·75

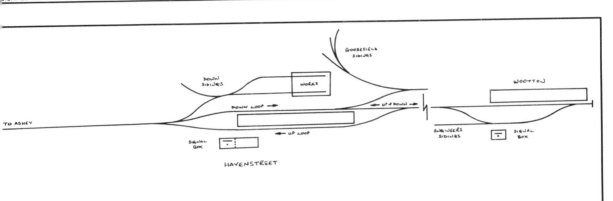

HAVENSTREET

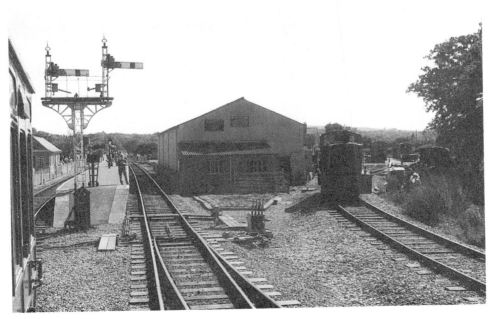

The layout of the station at Havenstreet is unusual in that the station buildings are not on the platform but, as the result of rebuilding following the installation of a passing loop in 1926, stand to the north of the line at ground level. In this British Railways' era scene, *Freshwater* awaits the off on the up line towards Ashey and Smallbrook Junction. *J. H. Aston*

The atmosphere of steam is as strong today at Havenstreet, the Headquarters of the Isle of Wight Steam Railway, as it ever was in days gone by, as this scene, with the IWSR's 'Terrier' *Newport* waiting to run around her train after arriving from Wootton on 26 September 1990, shows. The water tower is not an original Havenstreet structure; in former times it was located at the northern end of the down platform at Newport station.

Passengers on both trains watch closely as the exchange of tokens takes place. The starter signal in the distance for the down train from Ryde has already been pulled 'off'; meanwhile, the other Adams '02' hauled train on the up line waits for a clear road. Havenstreet signal box occupies the near end of the attractive station building, the staff entrance being through the small porch near to the ubiquitous fire-buckets. Note the 'Best Kept Station Award' seat next to the box — with lawnmower and watering can hidden behind it! *IWSR Collection*

I had to perch on the top of a set of stepladders to recapture the scene on 26 September 1990 and, although there is much to be seen that is unchanged from years gone by, careful examination will reveal many of the changes initiated by the IWSR. In addition to the Works, visible to the left of the tracks, one major addition is the refreshment room which, built in the same distinctive style as the old waiting room and signal box and opened in September 1982, is just discernable behind the water tower.

Ashey

IWCR Station:
Opened: 20 December 1875
Closed: 21 February 1966
IWSR Station:
Opened: 2 May 1993

OS Map Reference: SZ 578888

A Ryde-bound train pulls around the curve into Ashey on 11 April 1964, with the level crossing serving unmade Gate House Lane between it and the platform ahead. In earlier years a single long siding ran southwards from the loop (passing to the left of the trees where the faded gate stands) to a chalk quarry below Ashey Down; on race days, excursion train coaches were stabled there - some being utilised a temporary refreshment saloons! *IWSR Collection*

The new gates erected by the IWSR stand closer to the permanent way than the former BR ones, although the posts from the latter's gates still exist on the up side of the line. Here the public footpaths between East Ashey and Ashey Gate House meet that leading to Ashey Quarry Down - the one to the quarry following the path of the long-abandoned Ashey siding access, seen here on 28 March 1996, being via a stile rather than the old railway gate present in 1964.

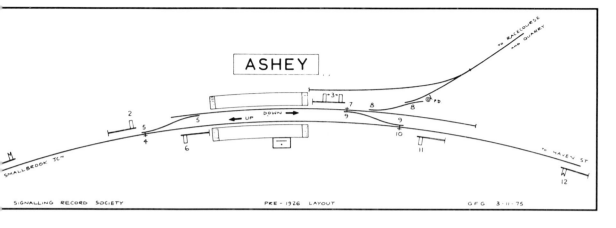

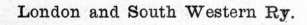

IWSR Collection

A 1950s view, with permanent way wagons standing in the old passing loop, taken out of service in 1926, and signs of weathering appearing on the roof of the station buildings, where fallen tiles have still to be replaced. Although Ashey was particularly busy on race days in the years preceding 1929 - when the local race-track's grandstand was gutted by fire and the course abandoned - a marked decline in passenger numbers set in in the 1930s and the station was reduced to unmanned halt status in the rationalisations on the Newport to Ryde line in 1953. *IWSR Collection*

On 28 March 1996 the single running line of the Isle of Wight Steam Railway passes through without any loop alongside it, although who knows if this might again be necessary at some future date if the restored railway's services continue to grow in popularity? Tasteful restoration has also been carried out on the former station house - now aptly named 'Old Station House'. In its garden one of the former Ashey station nameboards can still be seen from the footway between the level crossing and the current platform.

Part 3

Newport to Freshwater

Newport

FYNR Station:
Opened: 1 July 1913
Closed: mid-1923

OS Map Reference: SZ 499895

The exterior of the station building, with a respectable number of passengers making their way towards the booking hall, on the evening of 3 August 1965 (by which time, of course, the Freshwater line had already been closed). The steps leading up to the management offices are clearly visible, and note how all the parked vehicles bear the Isle of Wight 'DL' registration letters. Gubbins & Ball still play an important part in the Island's commercial life. *B. Sullivan*

Effectively changed beyond all recognition, this is the view up the station approach road on 10 March 1991; only an electricity sub-station bearing the title 'Station Approach' gives a clue to the hectic activity that once prevailed here. Perhaps, though, it is more than just a coincidence that the building that now stands where the station buildings once were (just out of camera to the right of the skip) is a funeral parlour!

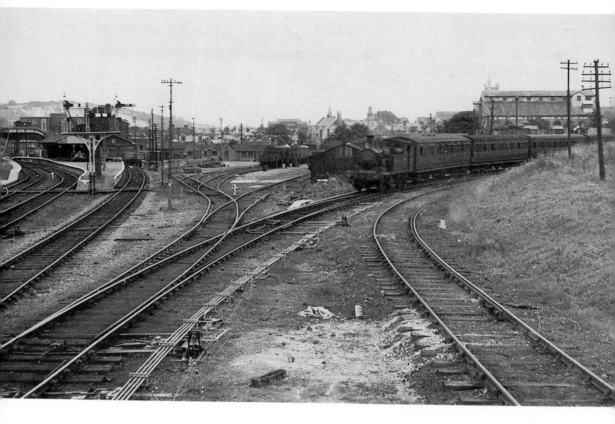

Having just crossed over the wrought iron and brick Towngate Viaduct, spanning Hunny Hill, running inbound from Freshwater during 1949, an unidentified Adams '02' pulls round the sharp curve at the end of the branch line before reversing into the 'Freshwater bay' at the north end of Newport station. Between the '02' and the station an assortment of goods wagons stand in the down sidings, to the left of which, behind the signal gantry, rises the white face of Shide Chalk Pit. *IWSR Collection*

The Newport by-pass and industrial estate access road alter the view today considerably. Although the brewery building has long gone, the two churches, the dome of the Town Hall and the more modern County Council building still provide good reference points on 30 June 1990. (Of the former viaduct, eight of the original nine brick arches remain; below them still stands the corrugated iron hut which was once the Offices of the FYNR and now finds good use as the Headquarters of the Island Branch of the Red Cross.)

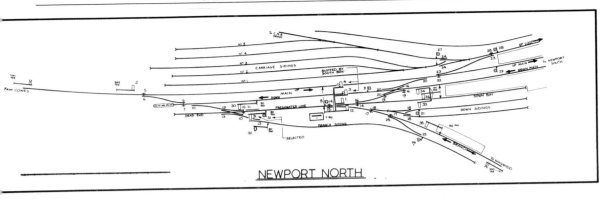

NEWPORT NORTH

SOUTHERN RAILWAY.

(9/46) 6M

Stock
787

TO

NEWPORT

(I. of W.)

IWSR Collection

115

Carisbrooke

Opened: 10 September 1888
Closed: 21 September 1953

OS Map Reference:
SZ 486885

Carisbrooke is badly in need of a spruce-up as the end of running approaches. The up platform loop, abandoned in 1927, is completely overgrown, and the down platform is very little better. It is hard to imagine that prior to the widespread introduction of buses, this was amongst the busiest of the Island stations, with many of the arriving or departing passengers being visitors to nearby Carisbrooke Castle. The 'crow stepping' on the gable ends and the circular capping tiles along the roof ridges match those to be found at other stations on the Newport to Freshwater line, a typical FYNR management gesture of giving character to its properties. *IWSR Collection*

Although Newport station has been completely razed to the ground, other signs of the railway era still give clues to the past. Thus, Carisbrooke gets my vote as the 'most changed' ex-railway location on the whole of the Island — on 9 May 1990 only a slight hump in the playing field of Archbishop King RC Middle School is left as evidence of what once stood here.

It is 1949, and this view is looking east back towards the junction at Newport, with the main line having just been relaid. The siding is well overgrown, although still officially 'in use'; however, after the war it saw even less traffic than the little it carried during the days of hostilities. *IWSR Collection*

Well-mown grass and modern housing to the left provide no connection with the 1949 view, but the housing on the right provides the link, although that on the hill at Whitepit Lane is masked by numerous trees.

Gunville Siding

OS Map Reference: SZ 479886

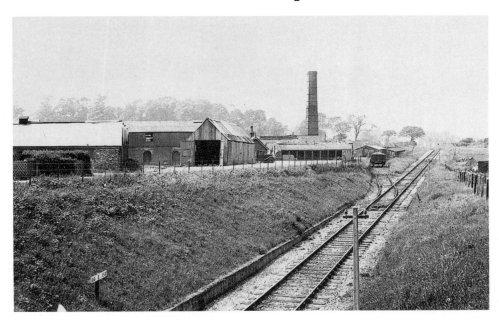

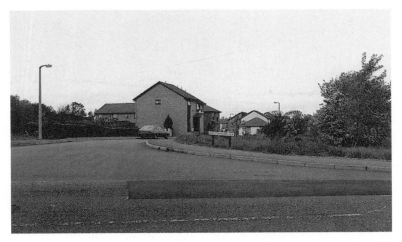

Located just to the west of Gunville Road overbridge, the five-wagon capacity siding served Gunville Brick Works, which produced tiles and glazed pottery, as well as basic bricks, until the 1940s. Operations here were typical of those nationwide in the first half of the 20th century: transportation out of manufactured goods, and in of raw materials or, as in the Gunville case, coal as a source of power. *Dr J. Mackett Collection*

Alvington Manor View Estate occupies the site on 9 May 1990 but, to the left of the houses, the brick works pit serves as a coarse fishing lake. Small parts of the overbridge retaining wall are still to be found on the east side of Gunville Road, together with a small number of fencing posts.

Watchingwell Halt

(Also known as
Upper Watchingwell Halt)

Opened: Prior to June 1897
Closed: 21 September 1953

OS Map Reference:
SZ 448884

How charming is this view of the once private halt, with milk churns on the platform, beautiful rural scenery and a general air of tidyness. Built later than the other stations on the Freshwater branch, Watchingwell was positioned to serve Swainston Estate, the domain of Southampton MP Sir John Barrington Simeon, and did not always appear in public timetables. *A. R. Sedgwick*

Only a particularly observant hiker along the course of the disused line will spot the halt today, for thick hedges mask from casual gaze the pretty home that it has been turned into. The platform remains in place and only a relatively small extension has been added to the original structure of this remote railway outpost. Happily, the house is also adorned with railway signs and other items of memorabilia.

The reciprocal view, looking down the single line on towards Calbourne, just under 2 miles further west. The track has recently been relaid, hence the clean ballast, the engineers' reference marks on the platform face and the pile of sleepers still awaiting collection. A short siding once led off to the south behind the platform, but the rails and associated pointwork have long been lifted. *IWSR Collection*

The foliage looking west is just as thick as that found when looking the opposite way and, again, no easy view of the station is available. Sadly, no '02s' or 'Terriers' pass this way any more, but the wideness of the trackbed is explained by its use as access to some of the local farms.

Near Watchingwell

OS Map Reference: SZ 438886

Taken at the 4½ milepost to the west of Watchingwell Halt, an unidentified Adams '02' runs bunker-first on the downhill gradient towards Calbourne. The beautiful countryside through which the train is passing is typical of that to be found in West Wight, and is seen here in the 1950s. *Pamlin Prints*

The line is completely overgrown and nature has reclaimed her own, but I was able to locate the site by measurement from the adjacent under and overbridges to the west and east respectively. Additionally, plenty of ash underfoot — once used as track ballast — indicated the new coppice's previous history.

Calbourne
(Also known as Calbourne and Shalfleet)

Opened 10 September 1888
Closed: 21 September 1953

OS Map Reference:
SZ 423883

The gates are closed to rail traffic in this view of the line coming in from Newport taken during British Railways days, but judging by the quite respectable number of passengers waiting to board the next train (probably up to Newport), they will soon be opening. Note, at the far end of the platform, the wood and corrugated iron ticket office, transferred here in Southern Railway days, after the squabbles over running rights at Newport station were finally resolved. *D. Priddle*

No hints whatsoever of days gone by are present from the same vantage point on 24 March 1991. The garden tub stands almost exactly where the group of three passengers stood in the earlier photograph, whilst the young trees beyond the decorative walling are located on the former trackbed.

A fascinating mixture of building styles and materials at the station, seen from the level
crossing on the minor road joining the villages of Shalfleet and Calbourne, both a full mile
distant from the station inconveniently sited to serve them. The seat on the platform slope
could hardly have been the most comfortable on the railway system, but at least it enjoyed
some overhead protection from the elements! *J. H. Aston*

All the old buildings have been demolished and a pleasant modern bungalow, 'Badgers
Bend', built on the site — even the attractive period lamp cannot claim railway parentage! The
left-hand of the two 'toadstools' marks the spot where the level crossing gatepost stood in the
earlier view.

Looking on towards Ningwood, the four-wheeled goods trolley and sacks of mail add an everyday touch to this 1949 view along the platform, with the single siding overgrown but still in use. The high ground in the distance is part of the beautiful Compton Down, near to Freshwater and the line's end. *IWSR Collection*

The goods trolley has been replaced by a wheelbarrow, and the trackbed turned into a neat stretch of garden. The platform edge still bears many traces of white paint and the drain cover, clearly visible in the earlier photograph, is still in situ in front of the greenhouse, but masked by the plants in this 12 June 1990 view.

Calbourne Viaduct

Looking back up the line towards Calbourne on 15 April 1950. Beyond the speed restriction board, Calbourne station's distant signal, topped by an 'open' LSWR finial, and a public crossing over the track are both clearly visible. *R. A. Silsbury Collection*

Barbed wire has replaced the SR single strands of fencing on 5 May 1990, but the old concrete posts still mark the field boundaries on either side of the trackbed. The direction signpost just visible at the end of the right-hand hedge marks out the public footpath from Newbridge to Shalfleet — still following the same course as in railway days.

Running north into the Solent from the slopes below Brightstone Forest, the Caul Bourne, to give it its correct name, is best known for providing the water element of picturesque 'Winkle Street' and for powering the still-working Calbourne Mill. Only a minor obstacle to the navvies laying the track out to West Wight from Newport, it was — as can be seen in this 1950 shot — easily crossed by means of an iron viaduct. *R. A. Silsbury Collection*

Only small amounts of brickwork have survived the ravages of time; the metalwork has long been taken away for scrap. As in the earlier photograph, this 5 May 1990 view is taken looking to the east.

Ningwood

Opened: 10 September 1888
Closed: 21 September 1953

OS Map Reference:
SZ 401883

Ningwood Station, looking towards Yarmouth, on 18 September 1953. A single passenger, looking slightly out of place at this remote rural station with his pin-stripe suit, bowler hat and briefcase, awaits the next service up to Newport. The water tank was placed here in the 1930s, and the crossing loop extended to 400 feet to allow longer trains — such as 'The Tourist' direct service from Ventnor to Freshwater — to pass. *J. H. Aston*

The platform edge and slope, near the site of the water tank, provide a firm link with the past, as does the hidden small platform shelter, now used as a useful garden store.

In the days soon after Nationalisation, the section staff is exchanged as an unidentified '02' pulls to a halt at the down platform, at the near end of which stands the Ningwood signal box. As the section staff is in use and the Ningwood box 'switched in', it can safely be assumed that this was a relatively busy day on the branch; on quieter days a 'long staff' was used and the box 'switched out'. The Station Master's house is visible behind the up waiting shelter and the water tank. *IWSR Collection*

The overbridge has been removed in the course of road re-alignment but, behind the shrubs growing out of the platform edge, the old Station Master's house still stands, now in private ownership. The down platform buildings have been converted into an attractive private residence.

Looking again towards Yarmouth, Adams '02' *Merstone* draws to a halt in the up crossing loop only a few weeks before closure. Despite the path being taken by the workman near the front coach, the official pedestrian right of way to the up platform was via a plank crossing at the other end of the station! *R. C. Riley*

The trackbed is still very obvious, happily never having been filled in. The wooden structures have been cleared away but the brick building survives, with a new lamp and a new source of power.

Yarmouth

Opened: 10 September 1888
Closed: 21 September 1953

OS Map Reference:
SZ 358895

Yarmouth station looking down the line towards Freshwater; the houses are in Station Road, and enjoyed views of the line from both back and front windows. Goods sidings once occupied the area behind the corrugated iron hut, but these have now ceased to operate and have already become overgrown. *J.H. Aston*

All signs of the houses in Station Road and the sidings are obscured by lush hedgerows on 12 June 1990 which, even to the non-rail enthusiast, help make this a particularly attractive part of the old railway system to explore. Even after all these years, the fact that a passing loop was once laid here is evidenced by the width of the footpath.

Alverstone eases to a halt with a down train on 10 September 1953, perhaps carrying passengers for the ferry to the mainland? Although plans have raised their heads over the years for a tunnel below, or a bridge above, the western end of the Solent, they have never really progressed beyond the initial planning stages — hence the small sign beneath the running-in board! With the sands of time rapidly running out for the Freshwater branch, the station still looks remarkably clean, tidy and efficient. Yarmouth once boasted a passing loop and two platforms, the down platform having to be built staggered from the up due to the course of Thorley Brook in the foreground. Traffic schedules never warranted the second platform and, together with the passing loop, it was abandoned in the 1920s. *R. C. Riley*

Converted to a Youth Centre, the station building on 5 May 1990 is little altered from its original design and is a credit to its present tenants, although the canopy has been removed and the chimneys lowered. Note the railings still in place over Thorley Brook. Today, passengers for the ferry service to Lymington arrive directly at the slipway by car or bus!

Less than a fortnight before closure, *Shorwell* pulls in across the brook with a train from Freshwater. Tennyson Down dominates the skyline, and notice the boats on the River Yar, along the eastern bank of which *Shorwell* has just travelled. *R. C. Riley*

Pedestrians exercising their dogs in this most attractive corner of the Garden Island on 5 May 1990 give movement to today's scene. Some fencing remains at the back of the platform, but the cart and trolley have long since gone for scrap. Even this long after abandonment, vestiges of white paint on the platform edging stones still cling to the surface.

Freshwater

Opened: 10 September 1888
Closed: 21 September 1953

OS Map References:
Station: SZ 344870
Causeway Crossing:
SZ 348872

The FYNR's locomotive No 2, a Stroudley 'Terrier' 0-6-0T, passes Causeway Crossing, half a mile out of the Freshwater terminus, with a train of four-wheel coaches. The crossing-keeper's wife's washing is soon to acquire a sooty hue! *R. A. Silsbury Collection*

The causeway has changed little over the years, although in SR days the light wire fencing was replaced with the more robust concrete variety. The keeper's cottage is now a private residence, and the trackbed to Yarmouth forms a delightful bridleway.

On 17 September 1953, just days before the closure of the line, *Alverstone* stands ready to run bunker-first to Newport with a three-coach train. This view shows to good effect the length of the single platform, extended at least four times during the station's existence, and the Island's weedkilling train stabled in the old cattle dock road. The signal box just visible behind the latter train was located at Newport in FYNR days, became a bus shelter after Freshwater Station closed, and is now fulfilling its original purpose **again** at the IWSR's Wootton Station (see page 101). *J. H. Aston*

Next to the aptly named 'End of the Line Café', a smart garden centre **occupi**es the eastern end of the station area. Note, to the right of the plants, the uprights from the station nameboard and gas lamp still standing in position at the old platform edge on 8 May 1990.

The front of the attractive station building in its final form in, despite the sign, British Railways days, and little changed by the passage of time since 1888. The variety of information on the notice boards would make fascinating reading — were it not for the fact that the right-hand notice on the left-hand board gives details of the withdrawal of services! *J. H. Aston*

Acorn Springs factory occupies the site on 8 May 1990, but not all traces of the earlier view have been eliminated, for railway fencing still stands below the large tree. The memorial stone in front of the car is not a momento of the FYNR: it bears the inscription 'Robert Hooke — Physicist, Scientist, Architect & Inventor. 1635-1703'.

Part 4

Newport to Sandown

Newport

For details see pages 89 and 113.

An unidentified IWCR 0-6-0 'Terrier' tank loco, with chalk wagons both ahead and behind, runs over Coppins Bridge, south of Newport Station, in September 1920, the year in which the structure had had to be rebuilt. Just beyond here, this line — from Sandown or Ventnor West, through Merstone — converged with the line from Ryde, before crossing the River Medina via a hand-operated drawbridge. (When it was necessary to open the bridge to allow a vessel to pass, the two separate sections of track were moved clear on rollers, the signal wires had to be disconnected and the fishplates unbolted before a clear passage was available. Then of course, the reverse was required — quite a lengthy and labour-intensive operation!) *R. A. Silsbury Collection*

The girder bridge was dismantled in 1960 and by 30 June 1990 the whole area has been redeveloped — as is readily apparent! An extensive roundabout system, filtering traffic on and off the Newport by-pass, now occupies the site, with small sections of the old river bridge parapets having been incorporated into the attractive garden that has been laid out between the carriageways.

Pan Lane Crossing

OS Map Reference: SZ 503889

For the period 6 October 1875 until 1 June 1879, Pan Lane was the temporary terminus of the IWCR's line from Sandown towards Newport. However, by the time of this early 1950s photograph, the through route had long been completed and here an unidentified '02' climbs away with a train for Sandown. Note the enthusiast behind the signal, which was unique on the Island in latter days in having both home and distant arms on the same post. *IWSR Collection*

The continuation of the Newport by-pass is aligned along the disused trackbed. Pan Lane itself is now called 'Furlongs' and is only a footpath from the site of the crossing-keeper's cottage towards the town centre. Because the new wall precluded an exact comparison, this 30 June 1990 shot is taken from a few yards to the left of the spot occupied by the original photographer.

Shide Chalk Pit

OS Map Reference: SZ 506881

Viewed from the boundary of the golf course, high up on St George's Down, the county town of Newport and distant Parkhurst Forest form an interesting backdrop to this 1936 view of Shide Chalk Pit, which was also known as Shide Quarry. The light, flat-bottomed rails of the sidings converge on the short tunnel, through which access was gained to the main line just north of Shide Station. *T. P. Cooper Collection*

Since workings ceased during the Second World War, nature has reclaimed much of her territory and, apart from the tunnel itself, traces of the past history of this spot were hard to find on 7 May 1990 — the buildings on the quarry floor having no connection with either the earlier workings or the railway.

An interesting shot inside the pit, full of fascinating detail, with a rake of open wagons standing on the quarry floor, from whence it will be pulled to either Cement Mills, with chalk for processing, or to other parts of the railway system with track ballast. Because of permanent way weight restrictions, only 'Terrier' tank locos were permitted entry to the pit. *Dr J. Mackett Collection*

Thick vegetation on the footpath leading into the pit, which is today a popular children's adventure area, precluded my obtaining the same camera angle as above. The different aspect, however, does not mask the complete change that the site has undergone.

Shide

Opened: 1 February 1875
Closed: 6 February 1956

OS Map Reference:
SZ 504864

Looking back from Shide station towards Newport and, for through trains, Cowes. The infant River Medina flows under the white-railed bridge beyond the nearer siding whilst, in the distance, an assortment of wagons stand in the overgrown sidings from which the line once led to the Chalk Pit. *IWSR Collection*

Major road re-routing, and the abandonment of this stretch of track, led to the river being culverted along the route of the permanent way with all traces of the railway being erased; however, on 7 May 1990 the footpath to Newport Town Centre still follows its original course on the left.

Nestling under St George's Down, just visible in the background, Shide was the terminus of the line from Sandown for most of the month of February 1875 whilst work was completed on the section up to the temporary Pan Lane Station (prior to Newport opening for traffic). In this view, the extra large station nameboard is well worthy of note. *Real Photographs/Ian Allan Ltd*

On 7 May 1990 no trace remains of the station buildings and, because of the re-routing of the river, I was unable to obtain an exact comparison shot from this direction; the wooden post and rail fencing in the foreground follows the line of the public footpath just discernable on the right-hand side of the earlier photograph.

In this 1949 view looking on towards Blackwater we see the porter/signalman preparing to open the crossing gates across Shide Road. As well as its main-line functions, the 9-lever signal box controlled access to the sidings and, prior to its closure in 1944, the track into Shide Chalk Pit. *IWSR Collection*

On 30 June 1990 traffic along Shide Road no longer runs the risk of delays at the crossing gates — in fact, there are no public level crossings left on the island. The local authorities have converted the trackbed to Blackwater into a cycle path, clearly seen beyond the new bridge. Note the unchanged line of pine trees on the horizon.

Blackwater

Opened: 1 February 1875
Closed: 6 February 1956

OS Map Reference:
SZ 507864

A respectable number of passengers await the arrival of this unidentified Adams '02', as it pulls in to the platform running bunker-first. However, I suspect that the many people leaning out of the coach windows are enjoying the ride and the scenery, rather than preparing to alight at Blackwater! The station house, which also contained the booking office, faces out on to the level crossing on the A3020 road from Newport to Shanklin. *R. A. Silsbury Collection*

Re-named 'Brambles', the station house has been enlarged to provide a family home, the extension being built over the ground previously occupied by part of the platform; note the merging of the old and new roof tiles. The greenhouse stands in front of where the shelter and toilets once were. How many casual observers, though, would connect this rural spot with the railways of the first half of the 20th century?

Looking towards the station from the A3020 in the early 1950s. Just three notice boards adorn the platform railings, but between the wars Blackwater was well known for its extensive collection of large and attractive enamel advertising signs. The tall 'cupboard' to the right of the waiting room housed a stretcher and first aid equipment, a feature to be found on nearly all of the Island's stations. *R. A. Silsbury Collection*

By 9 May 1990 the road has graduated to cat's-eyes and white markings! The remains of the platform can be seen to the right of the greenhouse and, of course, the size of the station house extension is very obvious.

Looking in a northerly direction from the goods yard, this scene of country station, waiting car and branch-line train pulling away evokes sweet memories of the days when steam ruled supreme and our railway system was the envy of the civilized world! *IWSR Collection.*

No need for the passing car to stop today; the railway has gone, and the former goods yard is the forecourt of a garage! Note, in both photographs, how the gradient of the road gives the false impression of the station house having a pronounced slope to it and, also, the cut-off level crossing gatepost (behind the buffer stop in the earlier photograph) still in position on 9 March 1991.

Merstone

Opened: 1 February 1875
Closed: 6 February 1956

OS Map Reference:
SZ 526845

A fine view of Merstone Station looking towards Newport in June 1950, showing a plethora of railway artefacts. Access to the platforms is direct from the road and via the slope between the railings; when built, subways below the rails led directly on to the platforms, but regular flooding led to their abandonment in the 1920s. *A. R. Sedgwick*

Sadly, on 6 May 1990 the site is in ruins, with all structures — apart from the platforms — at this once important junction demolished. No doubt it is now considered 'ripe for development'!

An evocative 1949 view of the junction, as *Shanklin* pulls in with a train from Sandown. Beyond the road crossing, the line to Ventnor West (see Part 5) can be seen diverging off to the right. Trains between Newport and Sandown always used this platform, except when two trains crossed here and both platforms were used. If a Ventnor West branch train was also present in the latter circumstances, it would be parked off the main line in the head shunt to the north of the station, where a small coaling stage was provided for the use of the branch locomotive. *R. C. Riley*

The discarded road works sign frames on the left mark where the platform railings once stood; save for the line of the track (which is now a private road called 'Newlands') and the edging stones in the middle of the picture, nothing else remains on 6 May 1990.

Little Budbridge
Near Merstone

OS Map Reference: SZ 535842

Open countryside between Merstone and Horringford, looking down Redstone Bank towards the latter, with track relaying just completed and new ballast dropped ready for lifting and packing. The occupation underbridge gave access between two of the fields belonging to Little Budbridge Farm. *R. A. Silsbury Collection*

The sides of the bridge are just visible in this view taken on 9 May 1990, open to the skies, for the bridge plates themselves were removed when the rails were lifted. Some concrete fence posts remain to the left of the embankment, and note the supported stanchion still in the field to the right of the much-matured tree.

Horringford

Opened: 1 February 1875   OS Map Reference:
Closed: 6 February 1956   SZ 543853

Viewed from the main road looking towards Merstone in the year prior to closure, the scene is one of smart tranquility. Sadly, Horringford — little used, but always tidy — was to be able to offer such thumbnail sketches of the romantic days of steam for no more than a few more months. The signal box controlled the level crossing over the A3056 Newport to Sandown Road, as well as access to the single siding. *R. A. Silsbury Collection*

On 7 May 1990 the wooden fence and extensive bushes prevent a view back along the old trackbed, and resurfacing of the road has removed any signs of the rails. Behind the fence, however, the stone bridge parapet still stands.

Looking, in June 1950, down the line towards Newchurch. The ladder leaning on the lower roof seems to be a semi-permanent fitting, for it appears in all the post-war photographs of Horringford that I have seen; I suspect it was used to give access for lighting the higher of the two platform oil lamps. *A. R. Sedgwick*

Changed considerably since being under railway management, two new dormer windows have been added to the house and the signal box has been removed. Note the concrete post at the extreme right-hand edge of the earlier photograph; it is the upright securing the station name, and its remains are just visible in the 5 May 1990 view. Today, the sign itself has found a final resting place amongst the memorabilia collected together at Havenstreet by the IWSR.

Newchurch

Opened: 1 February 1875
Closed: 6 February 1956

OS Map Reference:
SZ 559859

Bare trees and long shadows enhance this crisply clear view from the crossing gates, looking towards Alverstone, on the afternoon of 15 January 1956. Possessing a style of structure all of its own, the station building — built on the south side of the single track — was little more than a wooden hut, although a substantial station house had also once graced the site. I can't help thinking that the three fire buckets would have been woefully inadequate if a spark from the stove or a passing train had fallen in the wrong place! The SR concrete signal post is worthy of note: unusually, it is placed on the offside of the track. *L. Elsey*

Only the name of the modern bungalow — 'Newchurch Crossing' — gives an obvious clue to the previous activity at this site. There is, however, one further relic of railway days: the remains of the platform slope have been cleverly incorporated into a garden rockery, lying out of sight behind the hedge and just to the right of the bus stop in this 14 March 1991 view.

Alverstone

Opened: 1 February 1875
Closed: 6 February 1956

OS Map Reference:
SZ 577856

Taken on a wet afternoon in 1956, this view towards Sandown shows how a mill race ran below both the track and the platform — hence the stronger railings at the nearer end of the latter. A milepost in the 'V' between the main line and siding shows 1½ miles to the junction with the ex-IWR line at Sandown. *R. C. Riley*

To the right, all signs of the past — apart from the station house — have been eliminated on 7 May 1990. However, some of the old metal stanchions from the mill race bridge on the left still serve their original function, but now carrying new wires.

The fine station house on 22 January 1956, with the road bridge over the River Yar to the left. Note the pedestrian entrance gate, which led straight on to the platform slope, and the fine selection of official posters and timetables. The large station sign replaced a much smaller, wooden one which, before Nationalisation, faced the road and not the rails! *R. C. Riley*

Despite changes at ground floor level, on 7 May 1990 the house is still instantly recognisable as what it once was. Note, for example, the ornamental decor on the ridge of the roof. The crossing gates have been replaced by a far less impressive tubular steel gate and the trackbed now carries a bridleway and footpath, the latter back towards the site of Newchurch Station.

With a Vauxhall saloon waiting at the closed gates on a sunny afternoon in October 1951, *Shorwell* makes her way over the level crossing with a Newport to Sandown train. *C. G. Woodnut*

Not held up by any passing train on 7 May 1990, the Volvo stands where the Vauxhall waited nearly 40 years before. Note how much of the adjacent scenery has remained unchanged by the passage of time: the distant cottage, field gate, bridge parapet and, to a great extent, the station house.

Sandown

Opened: 23 August 1864
(See also page 50)

OS Map Reference:
SZ 593845

With Brading Down visible in the background, the former Isle of Wight (Newport Junction) Railway's track climbs up from the bed of the Yar Valley into Sandown station in this view from 1949. A single carriage stands in Brickfields siding — and note the informal 'Staff only' notice above the door to the wooden hut! *IWSR Collection*

The buffer from brake-van SR55724 can be seen on the left of the 12 June 1990 photograph, with Class '03' diesel 03179 in the headshunt. The track to Newport has long been lifted, and the wooden hut has been replaced with a more modern structure. The hand lever controls the nearer set of points, and an Annett's key the points connecting the siding to the main line — both were previously controlled by Sandown box.

Part 5

Merstone to Ventnor West

Merstone

Opened: 1 February 1875
Closed: 6 February 1956
(See also pages 149-151)

OS Map Reference:
SZ 526845

Early evening on 14 September 1953, and *Shorwell* pulls in to Merstone with the 5.08 pm train from Sandown to Newport. It is 12 months after the withdrawal of the service to Ventnor West, but the permanent way, off to the right, remains in place, whilst coaching stock from the former branch stands idle in the nearby siding. *J. H. Aston*

The most obvious sign of years gone by in this 6 May 1990 view — taken from the top of a pair of step ladders and not from the signal box window — is the graceful arch of the bridge in the middle distance, beside which stands Little Budbridge Farm (see page 152). A Southern Water facility stands where the Southern Railway once held sway!

Godshill

Opened: 20 July 1897
Closed: 15 September 1952

OS Map Reference:
SZ 522820

Taken in June 1950, this view of Godshill station shows that a small amount of milk traffic was still being handled and, although it had long been an unstaffed halt, it is pleasing to see how tidy the area was being kept. *A. R. Sedgwick*

On 6 May 1990 the platform buildings and the station house are both private residences, structurally little changed. Note the awning support brackets still in position at the front of the single storey building and the baulk of timber on the extreme right, marking where the single siding's buffer once stood.

Near Godshill

Freshwater pulls its two-coach train across the bridge over the minor road joining Godshill and Chale on 28 July 1951, with Whitwell the next stop. The driver has found time to admire the passing scenery — the beautiful valley of the infant River Yar. *Pamlin Prints*

The bridge itself has long gone, but small amounts of the brickwork parapets can still be found in the hedgerows on either side of the road. Much of the embankment between the bridge and the hamlet of Southford, on the northern edge of Whitwell village, has been dug away, levelled and returned to farming, as this 10 June 1990 view shows. I did, however, stumble across a rail chair screw whilst positioning the tripod for this photograph, and wondered how many times the plough had turned it over since the line was abandoned . . .

Whitwell

Opened: 20 July 1897
Closed: 15 September 1952

OS Map Reference:
SZ 522782

Whitwell station has been converted into a fine private residence and now bears the name 'Cartref'. Unfortunately, for personal reasons, the present occupants were unable to allow me access to take photographs, but were kind enough to send me this fine aerial view of the station, taken in the mid-1980s. Complemented by the photographs taken by Roger Silsbury on 2 August 1988, it is possible to fully appreciate the current status of this quiet, attractive location.

A fine view looking up the line back towards Godshill in November 1928, five years after Grouping and with the influence of the Southern Railway already evidenced by the concrete nameboards and fenceposts. Soon this influence would be even more apparent, with the removal of the passing loop, abandonment of the up platform and the dismantling of the signal box! *R. A. Silsbury Collection*

Although a west-facing conservatory has been added, and the platform canopy removed, there is no doubt whatsoever as to the original use of 'Cartref'. Note the canopy supports embedded in the wall of the single storey building and, quite unusual over such a span of years, the same pots still atop the chimney stacks. *R. A. Silsbury*

167

Dean Crossing, Whitwell

OS Map Reference: SZ 526771

The only level crossing on the Ventnor West branch lay ¼ mile north of St Lawrence Tunnel on the outskirts of the village of Whitwell, and took its name from the nearby Dean Farm. Most unusually for a completely rural location, the extravagance of a footbridge was provided for any pedestrian who might be delayed on finding the gates open to rail traffic! *R. A. Silsbury Collection*

Although all the other railway artefacts have long been removed from the site, the crossing-keeper's cottage has altered little over the years. The trackbed now provides access from the public road to the northern portal of the tunnel, inside which is located a mushroom farm.

St Lawrence

Opened:
20 July 1897
Closed:
15 September 1952

OS Map References:
Station: SZ 535767
Tunnel — North Portal: SZ 527769
South Portal: SZ 534767

Beyond the south end of the tunnel lies the single platform of St Lawrence station. Note the steep gradient down from the tunnel mouth, very evident. An unstaffed halt since 1927, no one has been on hand to tend the flower beds in recent years. *IWSR Collection*

A collection of second-hand cars stands on the filled-in trackbed on 6 May 1990, but surprisingly the flower beds are better looked after than in BR days! The steep slope under 'top cliff', as it is locally known, which was quite obvious in the earlier photograph, is now stablised by thick undergrowth, combating the slippage which often occurred in earlier years.

The temporary terminus of the branch from Merstone from 1897 to 1900, when the final 1½ miles of track to Ventnor Town, as it was then called, was opened, this 1930s view was taken after the short siding that once existed beyond the road bridge was lifted. Note the wooden nameboard and the predominately grass-surfaced platform. *IWSR Collection*

Although infilling has resulted in the necessity of a different camera angle, the origins of today's private house are obvious on 10 June 1990. The street lamp is still in situ, but the angle of lean has been reduced! The board below the left-hand house window gives passers-by details of the station's history, although the dates are slightly in error.

Ventnor West

(Known as
Ventnor Town until 1923)

Opened: 1 June 1900
Closed: 15 September 1952

OS Map Reference:
SZ 554772

This interesting 1928 view, complete with dog, shows the water tank, little-used No 2
platform, starting signals and the rather imposing box, typical of the excessive expenditure
made on the branch by its founders. Fitted with 13 levers, it was usually 'switched out' when
'one engine in steam' operations were in effect between here and Merstone Junction. *Pamlin
Prints*

Although I stood on the old platform to take this comparison shot on 10 June 1990, no
other railway remains can be seen looking in the up direction. Behind the hedge, however,
stands the station's old furniture repository and on wet days the word 'Pickfords' can still be
picked out on the roof.

In the early post-war years, 'Terrier' No W13 *Carisbrooke* — which once carried the number W3 — coasts past the water column and inspection pit siding, with a mid-day service from Merstone. Although not as marked as the amphitheatre atmosphere at the other Ventnor station, the effect produced by the surrounding mass of lush trees and vegetation at Ventnor West was not dissimilar. *D. Priddle*

A contrast in weather as well as scenery! A thick sea mist, so typical of the southern Island coastline, rolls over Castle Close and envelops the spot where *Carisbrooke* stood nearly half a century ago. On 14 March 1991 the embankment behind the water column is still as prominent a feature as ever, and only a cursory search is needed to locate the flattened area where the siding passed below it.

The station displays the name 'Ventnor', but was originally titled Ventnor Town, and was known as Ventnor West after Grouping in 1923. Too far out of the town to compete with the more centrally located terminus of the ex-IWR line from Ryde, the station, in common with all others between here and Merstone, was never a commercial success. *IWSR Collection*

Although the station house and most of the adjacent main buildings are still standing on 10 June 1990, and in use as a private residence, all other traces of the railway past have been buried below the pleasant bungalows that now face on to Castle Close.

Appendices

Appendix 1:
Chronological list of events

1845   Newport Town Council meets and decides to go ahead with plans for a railway from Cowes to Newport - the Island's first railway.

1862   On 16 June the first passenger train to run on the Isle of Wight leaves Cowes at 8.15 am for the 4½-mile run to Newport, on the Cowes & Newport Railway (C&NR).

1864   The line is opened to passenger traffic from Ryde (now Ryde St John's Road) towards Shanklin. The first tram services commence on Ryde Pier.

1866   The first through trains run from Ryde to Ventnor, the last part of the journey being through the Island's longest tunnel, 1,312 yards (1,200 m) long, under St Boniface Down.

1871   A horse-drawn tram link is established between Ryde Pierhead and Ryde station.

1875   Ryde linked to Cowes, via Newport - where a new station is opened to accommodate the two railways.

1880   The Joint Committee of the London & South Western and the London, Brighton & South Coast railways opens its pier at Ryde, with the railway connection finally established between Ryde St John's Road and Ryde Pierhead, via the new Ryde Esplanade Station.

        The line from Sandown finally reaches Newport, having initially terminated at Shide in 1875 and Pan Lane in 1879.

        The Cowes & Newport Railway and Ryde & Newport Railway Joint Committee takes over the running of the Isle of Wight (Newport Junction) Railway.

1882   The branch line to Bembridge, from Brading, opens to traffic.

1887   The Isle of Wight Central Railway Company (IWCR) is formed, consisting of the original Cowes & Newport, Ryde & Newport and Isle of Wight (Newport Junction) Railways.

1897   The Newport, Godshill & St Lawrence Railway (NGSLR) opens its line towards Ventnor West as far as St Lawrence.

1889   The line from Freshwater to Newport is opened to passenger traffic, having been opened to freight traffic the previous year. The IWCR operates this line on behalf of the FYNR.

1899   The Brading Harbour Railway is taken over by the Isle of Wight Railway (IWR).

1900   The final stretch of railway on the Isle of Wight, from St Lawrence to Ventnor West, is opened to traffic.

1913   Following a series of disagreements with the IWCR over the working of the Freshwater to Newport line, the Directors of the FYNR take over its working for themselves.

The NGSLR is taken over by the IWCR.

1923   **Grouping.** The IWR and IWCR are amalgamated on 1 January to form part of the new Southern Railway system; however, the FYNR remains independent until being forced into amalgamation on 1 August.

1948   **Nationalisation.** The Southern Region of British Railways assumes responsibility for the Island's railway system.

1952   Closure of the line from Merstone Junction to Ventnor West.

1953   Closure of the Newport to Freshwater line, the Brading to Bembridge branch, and Whippingham and Wootton stations.

1956   Closure of the Newport to Sandown line.

1966   Closure of the line from Cowes to Newport and Ryde (Smallbrook Junction), and from Shanklin to Ventnor. The end of main-line steam operation on the Isle of Wight.

1967   Electrification of the line from Ryde Pierhead to Shanklin and introduction of ex-London Transport Underground rolling-stock.

1971   The Isle of Wight Steam Railway (IWSR) commences operations on the Havenstreet to Wootton section of the old Newport to Ryde line, with plans to connect with the BR network at Smallbrook Junction.

1987   The first new station since the turn of the century is opened at Lake, to serve the growing community between Sandown and Shanklin.

1991   Opening of the IWSR's extension, via Ashey, to an interchange station with BR at Smallbrook Junction. The last of the 1923-24 vintage ex-London Transport stock is taken out of service.

1994   Network SouthEast is disbanded on 31 March under the Government's rail privatisation plans; Island Line trains are now operated by The Island Line Train Operating Unit Ltd, with Railtrack plc exercising the same role as elsewhere on mainland UK regarding permanent way, signalling and stations.

1995   The IWSR is chosen as 'Independent Railway of the Year'.

1996   The IWSR celebrates its 25th anniversary.

A feasibility study is published in January on the reactivation of a railway link between Shanklin and Ventnor, via Wroxall. The preferred option is for a single-line, third-rail system, following the former trackbed and with a cut-and-cover tunnel under part of Wroxall village. The recommendation is for through trains to be re-introduced between Ryde Pierhead and Ventnor.

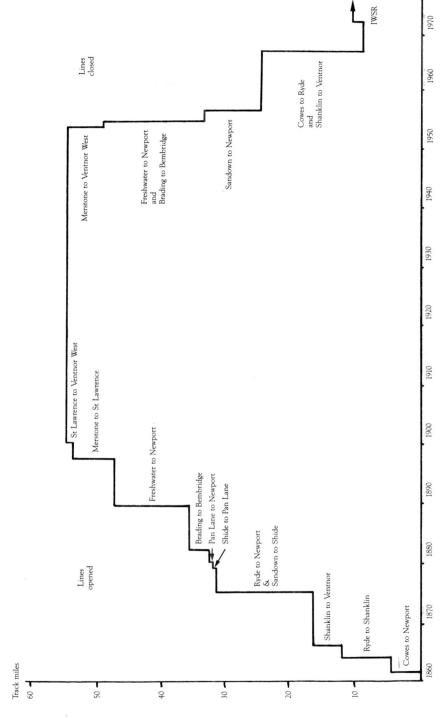

Chart portraying the expansion and contraction of railway track mileage on the Isle of Wight

Appendix 2:
List of IOW locomotives carrying Island placenames

With the exception of some of the earliest locomotives used by the Isle of Wight Central Railway, Island town and village names have traditionally been used to name Island-based locomotives. The majority of the names used were of places directly associated with the railway; however, Bonchurch, Chale, Osborne, Seaview, Shorwell and Totland were remote from the railway system, and Fishbourne's association was only through the ferry service.

This table shows the specific use of these local names over the years; it should be noted that in a few cases the locomotives listed did not always carry both the name and the associated number at the same time.

Name	Class	Number	To Island	Disposal
Ashey	Adams '02' 0-4-4	W28	1926	Scrapped 1967
Alverstone	Adams '02' 0-4-4	W29	1926	Scrapped 1966
Bembridge	Manning Wardle 0-6-0	Not numbered	1882	To War Department for service in Mesopotamia
	Stroudley 'Alx' 0-6-0	W4, then W14	1929	To mainland 1936
	Adams '02' 0-4-4	W33	1936	Scrapped 1967
Bonchurch	Beyer Peacock 2-4-0	Not numbered W18	1883	Scrapped 1928
	Adams '02' 0-4-4	W32	1928	Scrapped 1965

Name	Class	Number	To Island	Disposal
Brading	Beyer Peacock 2-4-0	Not numbered W17	1876(?)	It is possible that this loco could have been used on the Island by contractors from 1863-1872, later to become St Helens. Scrapped 1926
	Adams '02' 0-4-4	W22	1924	Scrapped 1967
Carisbrooke	Stroudley 'Alx' 0-6-0	W3, then W13	1927	To mainland 1949
	Adams '02' 0-4-4	W36	1949	Scrapped 1965
Calbourne	Adams '02' 0-4-4	W24	1925	To IWSR 1967
Chale	Adams '02' 0-4-4	W31	1927	Scrapped 1967
Cowes	Beyer Peacock 2-4-0	IWC4	1876	Scrapped 1925
	Brighton 0-6-0	IWC10	1900	To mainland 1936
	Adams '02' 0-4-4	W15	1936	Scrapped 1956
Fishbourne	Stroudley 'Alx' 0-6-0	W9	1930	To mainland 1936
	Adams '02' 0-4-4	W14	1936	Scrapped 1967
Freshwater	Stephenson 0-6-0		1886	Contractor's loco. To mainland c1890.
	Stroudley 'A1' 0-6-0	FYN2 W2, then W8	1913	To mainland 1949 To IWSR 1979.
	Adams '02' 0-4-4	W35	1949	Scrapped 1967
Godshill	Adams '02' 0-4-4	W25	1925	Scrapped 1963
Medina	Manning Wardle 0-6-0	FYN1	1913	Scrapped 1932
	Stroudley 'E1' 0-6-0	W1	1932	Scrapped 1957
Merstone	Adams '02' 0-4-4	W27	1926	Scrapped 1967
Mill Hill	Black Hawthorn 0-4-2	IWC3	1870	To mainland 1918
Newport	Hawthorn 2-2-2	IWC6	1875	Scrapped 1895
	Stroudley 'A1' 0-6-0	IWC11	1902	To mainland 1947. To IWSR 1974.
	Adams '02' 0-4-4	W34	1947	Scrapped 1955
Ningwood	Adams '02' 0-4-4	W18	1930	Scrapped 1966
Osborne	Beyer Peacock 2-4-0	IWC5	1876	Scrapped 1926
	Adams '02' 0-4-4	W19	1923	Scrapped 1955

Name	Class	Number	To Island	Disposal
Ryde	Beyer Peacock 2-4-0	Not numbered	1864	
		W13		Scrapped 1940
	Stroudley 'E1' 0-6-0	W3	1932	Scrapped 1959
Sandown	Beyer Peacock 2-4-0	Not numbered	1864	Scrapped 1923
	Adams '02' 0-4-4	W21	1924	Scrapped 1966
Seaview	Adams '02' 0-4-4	W17	1930	Scrapped 1967
Shanklin	Beyer Peacock 2-4-0	Not numbered	1864	
		W14		Scrapped 1927
	Adams '02' 0-4-4	W20	1923	Scrapped 1967
Shorwell	Adams '02' 0-4-4	W30	1926	Scrapped 1965
St Helens	Unknown class 2-4-0	Not numbered	c1881 (or 1863)	Contractor's loco. Sold in 1893 to contractor for the Newport, Godshill & St Lawrence Railway. Renamed *St Lawrence*. (See also *Brading*)
St Lawrence	Unknown class 2-4-0	Not numbered	c1881 (or 1863)	See above. Scrapped 1898
Totland	Adams '02' 0-4-4	W23	1925	Scrapped 1955
Whippingham	Beyer Peacock 4-4-0	IWC7	1906	Scrapped 1926
Whitwell	Adams '02' 0-4-4	W26	1925	Scrapped 1966
Wroxall	Beyer Peacock 2-4-0	Not numbered	1872	
		W16		Scrapped 1933
	Stroudley 'E1' 0-6-0	W4	1933	Scrapped 1960
Ventnor	Beyer Peacock 2-4-0	Not numbered	1868	
		W15		Scrapped 1925
	Stroudley 'A1' 0-6-0	IWC12	1903	To mainland 1936
	Adams '02' 0-4-4	W16	1936	Scrapped 1967
Yarmouth	Stroudley 'E1' 0-6-0	W2	1932	Scrapped 1956

Appendix 3:
Surviving coach bodies on the Island

A remarkable collection of withdrawn coach bodies and, to a much lesser extent, goods wagon bodies is to be found scattered around the Island, the largest number being 11 set together on the Duver at St Helens. I am most grateful to amateur historian and artist Don Vincent, of Apse Heath, Sandown, for the following selection of photographs, together with the distribution map showing where their final resting places are.

An ex-Metropolitan Railway coach, which became IWR coach No 5 on shipment to the Island in 1905, in use as a pair of beach huts below the St Helens Old Church Seamark on the Duver.

Now utilised as a store shed for a private house at Woodside, this body began its working life as the FYNR's coach No 6, being acquired as new stock from the makers.

Another ex-Metropolitan Railway coach, of the non-corridor, eight-compartment variety. Withdrawn from use in the late 1920s, it now resides at Gurnard as an angling club headquarters.

This beach hut on St Helens Duver, owned by the Medina Borough Council, saw service as a six-compartment coach with the Metropolitan Railway before being shipped to the Isle of Wight.

In use as a holiday chalet at Thorness Bay, this ex-LB&SCR three-compartment saloon coach — numbered 7996 by the Southern Railway — is unusual in having 'duckets' (guard's lookout windows) at both ends. Could it, possibly, at some time have been used for push-pull operations?

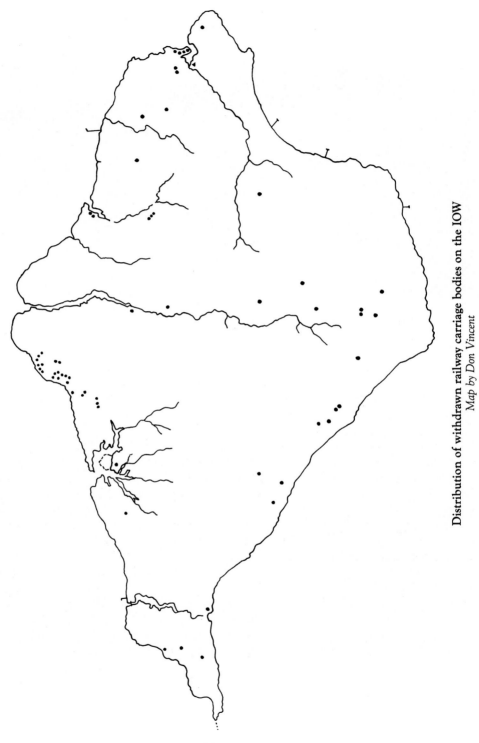

Distribution of withdrawn railway carriage bodies on the IOW
Map by Don Vincent

Appendix 4:
The status of the lines today
(Written jointly with Roger Silsbury)

Ordnance Survey source maps
1:50,000   Sheet 196 'Solent and The Isle of Wight'
1:25,000   Sheet SZ49/59 'Cowes'
               Sheet SZ28/38 and part of SZ48 'Western Wight'
               Sheet SZ58/68 and part of SZ48 'Newport (Isle of Wight)'
               Sheet SZ47/57 'Isle of Wight (South)'

The Isle of Wight is well known for its large number of well-signposted footpaths and bridleways and for its popularity with the walking fraternity. Thus it will come as no surprise to the reader to find that many parts of the abandoned railways are readily accessible today, for walking, cycling, riding, and for appreciating the beauty of the 'Garden Island' from the vantage points once enjoyed by those who rode upon the Isle of Wight Railways. Whilst exploring these paths and byways, railway artefacts will often be spotted: fencing, with stanchions of concrete, metal, cut-down sleepers or lengths of rail; discarded fishplates, rail chairs and screws; culverts with iron railings still in place; 'kissing gates' and farm access gates; pieces of bridge parapets and abutments; and remains of signal post bases, etc. The list is extensive — indeed, only the trains themselves and the smell of hot oil and steam are missing, and in many cases very little imagination is needed to conjure these up from the atmosphere that still lingers on!

A word of two of warning is, however, appropriate. First, the section of line between Ryde and Shanklin is in regular use by British Rail trains. It is **electrified** and **dangerous**. Apart from normal access to station platforms, the line is not open to the general public in any way whatsoever. Second, much of the abandoned trackbed is in private hands, as are all of the station buildings that have been converted into private residences. Please respect this privacy.

The description of the lines today follows the same order as the stations, etc in the main text. Ordnance Survey references are given only where not quoted earlier in the main body of the book.

187

Part 1a: Ryde Pierhead to Ventnor

The line from Ryde Pierhead to Shanklin is operated by British Rail's Network SouthEast 'Island Line', using ex-LRT electrically powered rolling-stock. However, parcels of land have been sold off by BR as follows:

Ryde St John's Road: the site of the locomotive running shed and up yard is now a builder's yard.

Sandown: the down yard has been developed as a housing estate.

Shanklin: a car park has been established on the site of the disused down yard.

Beyond Shanklin Station the line has been lifted, the Landguard Road underbridge having been removed and the station shortened at the Ventnor end. The embankment leading out from the station has been graded to provide an access road to Lower Hyde Holiday Park, but thereafter the trackbed is a bridleway to just short of Wroxall Station at SZ 550880. Part of Wroxall Station is now a light industrial site, the remainder being utilised as an access road and car park for new housing developed in the area. From SZ 553797 the trackbed has been reclaimed for agricultural use for about a quarter of a mile, before reverting to nature as it approaches Manor Road Bridge. Ventnor Tunnel is owned and maintained by Southern Water, whilst Ventnor Station is a busy light industrial site.

Part 1b: Brading to Bembridge

After leaving Brading Station a public footpath initially follows the abandoned trackbed as far as the site of the old Cement Mills in Wall Lane (SZ 614873), where the crossing cottages have been tastefully converted to a private house. This is the site of the end of the original siding to Brading Quay, from which access to the sea was lost following the land reclamation works associated with the Brading Harbour & Railway Company's extension to Bembridge, completed in 1882. From here the trackbed is used as a farm lane, past Bexley Point (SZ 618878) and on as far as the site of the single Carpenters Siding (SZ 622883), after which the line has been reclaimed for agricultural use. St Helens Station is a private residence, while St Helens Quay is a marina housing development, with yachting facilities in the modernised harbour. After crossing the River Yar, the next 1,000 yards or so of trackbed form a private farm track, and the final stretch towards, and including, Bembridge Station is a housing development.

Part 2: Cowes to Smallbrook Junction

The site of Cowes Station is under active development at the time of writing (spring 1991), and from Granville Road Bridge (SZ 494959) to St Mary's Road Bridge (SZ 494958) the track has been infilled and now forms gardens for the older houses, with some new housing having been developed as well. Granville Road Bridge is no longer a bridge — the roadway has been widened and the bridge itself demolished. A linear garden leads to Mill Hill Tunnel, where the local gun club has its headquarters and firing range, and continues to the south of the tunnel until reaching a new building used by a health club.

The stretch of trackbed past Smithards Lane Crossing is in private ownership, as is the busy Medina Wharf, but the rest of the line as far as Newport is a cyclepath and bridleway, passing *en route* the few remains of the halts at Medina Wharf and Cement Mills and the viaduct over Mill Pond.

Virtually all traces of Newport Station itself have disappeared under industrial development and road expansion. Minor traces of the drawbridge abutments remain at river level and some kerbing on the station approach road is detectable, near the electrical sub-station which still bears the designator 'Station Approach'.

From the east side of the dual carriageway the line to Fairlee is a public footpath, including the section through Newport Tunnel (SZ 503894), and beyond here farm access tracks are orientated where the rails once ran. Fattingpark Bridge (SZ 530915) has been demolished, Whippingham Station is a private residence, and the final quarter of a mile up to Station Road, Wootton, has fully reverted to nature.

The section of line from Wootton to Smallbrook Junction, via Havenstreet, is the domain of the Isle of Wight Steam Railway, with public access being restricted to the IWSR's stations: Wootton, Havenstreet, Ashey and Smallbrook Junction. From Ashey Station a public footpath leads south along the former quarry siding trackbed towards the chalk pit below Ashey Down (SZ 575880).

Part 3: Newport to Freshwater

The beginning of the old FYNR line is an access road to an industrial unit, also serving as a public footpath. The path diverges to the left, away from the line of the trackbed, and runs below the remaining eight brick arches of the Towngate Viaduct; the iron parts of the viaduct have long been scrapped, the western approach embankment having been incorporated into an industrial estate.

From the footpath at SZ 494894 to Petticoat Lane Crossing (SZ 493893), where the keeper's cottage still stands, the land is in private ownership; the next 300 yards also are in use as a footpath, then traces of the line disappear under the gardens of more new houses. Carisbrooke Station no longer stands, the site being part of a school playing field, and modern houses lie alongside the trackbed as far as the Gunville Road overbridge, where small sections of retaining wall are still to be found. Gunville Siding has been completely built over, and thereafter the trackbed has mainly returned to nature as far as Betty Haunt Lane Bridge (SZ 462887) which, with railway telephone insulators still in position on either side of the arch, continues to carry road traffic over the old line. Westwards, until adjacent to the farm at Great Park, all signs of the railway have been lost to farming, but at SZ 455883 the concrete abutments of Great Park Bridge, which carried the FYNR over a farm track, remain, and the old footpath from here to Watchingwell has been diverted to follow the trackbed itself.

Watchingwell Halt is a private house, and beyond that the line is a farm track for 1 mile, then completely overgrown as far as Pound Crossing (SZ 428885), where the crossing keeper's cottage remains as an attractive residence, together with two of the original crossing gate posts. Farmland predominates as far as Calbourne Station, where a modern bungalow has replaced the old buildings, and further farm tracks and stretches abandoned to nature continue, past the dismantled Calbourne Viaduct, as far as Ningwood Station. Here the overbridge has been demolished and the embankments levelled in a road improvement scheme; the station buildings remain, however, much improved and, again, converted for private use.

Continuing westwards, the trackbed is a mixture of farm track, absorption into adjacent fields and reversion to nature as far as Hill Place Crossing (SZ 375892), the final 200 yards prior to the crossing being part of a public footpath. Between Hill Place Crossing and Thorley Bridge (SZ 364896) the line has been obliterated completely under farmland, but from the bridge almost as far as Freshwater Station the trackbed forms a most attractive bridleway, passing Yarmouth Station — now a youth club — and Causeway Crossing, where the keeper's cottage is a private residence. The bridleway diverges from the old line as Freshwater Station is approached, the area now supporting a factory unit, garden centre and the End of the Line Café.

Part 4: Newport to Sandown

Almost all traces of the old Coppins Bridge and associated viaducts have disappeared under road schemes, including the southward extension of the Newport Eastern Relief Road (St Georges Way). Pan Mill (SZ 503889) still stands, now attractively converted into suites of offices, but with the 'Leigh Thomas & Co Ltd' sign still clearly visible on the brickwork. Half a mile or so from Newport the road veers slightly to the east of the trackbed and the canalised River Medina takes over as far as Shide Station, where a National Tyre Service Centre holds sway. The nearby Shide Pit is now a public open space, entry being via a footpath off Burnt House Lane. The tunnel, at the quarry end, is still very much in evidence, although gated off, but the access track from the main line to the other end has been filled in and used as the link road feeding off St Georges Way towards St George's Down.

The section between Shide and Blackwater is now a cycle route and footpath, stopping just short of the latter station, which is in private hands. Beyond the main road (A3020), the former goods yard is part of a garage forecourt and thereafter the line as far as Merstone, which is a County Council Depot, is in use as an unofficial footpath. South of the station a short stretch of the track has been converted to a private cul-de-sac, leading to bungalows on the site of the former Station Master's house and goods yard and to a Southern Water facility. Beyond the junction with the Ventnor West line, farm utilisation has taken over the land as far as Budbridge Lane overbridge (SZ 530842), after which the line has reverted to nature as it makes its way down the former Redway Bank, alongside the River Yar, towards Horringford — a private residence.

From here to Newchurch, where a bungalow has been built on the former station site, the line has been dedicated as a bridleway. Eastwards the low embankment continues across marshy ground to Alverstone, this section of the trackbed also being designated as a public right of way. Beyond the private house that once was home to the Station Master and his family, the embankment continues south-eastwards as an unofficial right of way as far as Longwood Lane and Alverstone Station, where, after skirting Fairway Caravan Park, the final 300 yards or so of the trackbed has been obliterated by a large housing development. However, even now a few fence-posts delineating ex-railway land still remain standing.

Part 5: Merstone to Ventnor West

From the junction at Merstone to Bow Bridge (SZ 524826) the trackbed is traceable but overgrown. Bow Bridge itself, on the outskirts of Godshill village, was demolished as part of a road widening scheme; immediately southwards, housing covers the line before, beyond the village, farmland again takes over. Godshill Station forms two private residences, and farm buildings occupy the former goods yard.

From Godshill to Roud Lane (SZ 519806) the line has been incorporated into adjacent farmland, although the abutments of Beacon Alley Bridge (SZ 521812) still remain. The line down to Southford Bridge (SZ 518792) has reverted to nature, with a short stretch at SZ 519801 incorporated into a footpath, and two sections of embankment, centred around SZ 519796 and adjacent to the former Southford Bridge, removed. From here the line disappears under grassland as far as an occupation underbridge, still standing, at SZ 519789, thereafter reverting to nature once more and passing under another occupation overbridge (SZ 521786) before reaching Whitwell Station, another private residence.

Beyond the removed Nettlecombe Lane Bridge the trackbed has returned to its natural state as far as Dean Crossing, where the keeper's cottage is in private use; from there it forms the access track to the mushroom farm established within St Lawrence Tunnel. Beyond the southern portal the line reverts to nature for a short while, but eastwards from St Rhadegund's footpath (SZ 532765) new housing covers the trackbed almost as far as St Lawrence Station, where again a conversion to private use has taken place. The overbridge carrying St Lawrence Shute remains; eastwards a road — Fishers — serving new housing follows the line for 300 yards, before nature again takes over.

The abutments of an occupation underbridge at SZ 540769 remain, after which the line forms a footpath for some 600 yards or so before becoming Castle Close, which fronts on to new houses all the way to the site of Ventnor West Station, again a fine private dwelling place.

Bibliography

Books consulted include:

Allen, P. & Macleod, A. *Rails in the Isle of Wight*, George Allen & Unwin Ltd (1967)

Blackburn, A. & Mackett, J. *The Railways and Tramways of Ryde*, Town & Country Press (1971)

Blackburn, A. & Mackett, J. *Freshwater, Yarmouth and Newport Railway*, Forge Books (1988)

Bradley, D.L. *A Locomotive History of Railways on the Isle of Wight*, The Railway Correspondence and Travel Society (1982)

Britton, A. *Once Upon a Line* (Volume One), Oxford Publishing Co (1983)

Britton, A. *Once Upon a Line* (Volume Two), Oxford Publishing Co (1984)

Fairclough, A. & Wills, A. *Southern Steam on the Isle of Wight*, Bradford Barton (1975)

Haye, P. *Steaming Through the Isle of Wight*, Middleton Press (1988)

Mitchell, V. & Smith, K. *South Coast Railways — Ryde to Ventnor*, Middleton Press (1985)

Mitchell, V. & Smith, K. *Branch Lines to Newport*, Middleton Press (1985)

Paye, P. *Isle of Wight Railways Remembered*, Oxford Publishing Co (1984)

Paye, P. & Paye, K. *Steam on the Isle of Wight (1956-1966)*, Oxford Publishing Co (1979)

Whittington, C. *Railways in the Isle of Wight*, G.G. Saunders & Co Ltd (1972)